"Hlinko is one of those guys who has figured out how to actually get some use out of the Internet, whether by tapping into heretofore unidentified fund-raising pools, getting a political message out to people who typically ignore political messages, or poking a pointed stick in the Establishment's eye." —Gersh Kuntzman, Newsweek.com

"Quite honestly, Hlinko is the best at what he does. Plus, he's got a sense of humor that rivals at least three of his other senses. . . . Four stars!" —Kevin Bleyer, writer, *The Daily Show with Jon Stewart*

"Gore might have invented the Internet, but John figured out how to make it work." —Suzie O'Hair, start-up adviser

"John Hlinko has pushed the envelope when it comes to ground-breaking strategies to attract, engage, and activate grassroots supporters." —Mike McCurry, former White House spokesman

"John Hlinko stepped forward to help us at MoveOn.org when we were just getting going. He's always an inspiration, bringing a deeply creative approach to everything he does."
—Joan Blades, cofounder, MoveOn.org and MomsRising.org

"[One of world's top 25] individuals, organizations, and companies that are having the greatest impact on the way the Internet is changing politics." —World Forum on e-Democracy

"He is one of the first people I think of when needing some creative ideas, some grassroots fire, and some technology expertise. That's a pretty damn good endorsement, and I mean every word of it."
—Donnie Fowler, campaign manager, Wes Clark for President, and national field and delegates director, Gore 2000

"Whether inside the box or out, John knows how to cook up dishes of information that are fun, irresistible, and nutritious. His advice has been invaluable as we've grown Blogads."
—Henry Copeland, founder, Blogads.com

shareretweetrepeatshareretweet
repeatshareretweetrepeatshare
retweetrepeatshareretweetrepeat

SHARE RETWEET REPEAT

Get Your Message Read and Spread

JOHN HLINKO

PRENTICE HALL PRESS

PRENTICE HALL PRESS
Published by the Penguin Group
Penguin Group (USA) Inc.
375 Hudson Street, New York, New York 10014, USA
Penguin Group (Canada), 90 Eglinton Avenue East, Suite 700, Toronto, Ontario M4P 2Y3, Canada (a division of Pearson Penguin Canada Inc.) • Penguin Books Ltd., 80 Strand, London WC2R 0RL, England • Penguin Group Ireland, 25 St. Stephen's Green, Dublin 2, Ireland (a division of Penguin Books Ltd.) • Penguin Group (Australia), 250 Camberwell Road, Camberwell, Victoria 3124, Australia (a division of Pearson Australia Group Pty. Ltd.) • Penguin Books India Pvt. Ltd., 11 Community Centre, Panchsheel Park, New Delhi—110 017, India • Penguin Group (NZ), 67 Apollo Drive, Rosedale, Auckland 0632, New Zealand (a division of Pearson New Zealand Ltd.) • Penguin Books (South Africa) (Pty.) Ltd., 24 Sturdee Avenue, Rosebank, Johannesburg 2196, South Africa
Penguin Books Ltd., Registered Offices: 80 Strand, London WC2R 0RL, England

While the author has made every effort to provide accurate telephone numbers and Internet addresses at the time of publication, neither the publisher nor the author assumes any responsibility for errors or for changes that occur after publication. Further, the publisher does not have any control over and does not assume any responsibility for author or third-party websites or their content.

First edition: January 2012

Library of Congress Cataloging-in-Publication Data

Hlinko, John.
  Share, retweet, repeat : get your message read and spread / John Hlinko.—1st ed.
    p. cm.
  Includes bibliographical references and index.
  ISBN 978-0-7352-0461-4
  1. Internet marketing.   2. Online social networks.   I. Title.
  HF5415.1265.H55 2011
  658.8'72—dc23   2011035712

PRINTED IN THE UNITED STATES OF AMERICA

10 9 8 7 6 5 4 3 2 1

Most Prentice Hall Press books are available at special quantity discounts for bulk purchases for sales promotions, premiums, fund-raising, or educational use. Special books, or book excerpts, can also be created to fit specific needs. For details, write: Special Markets, Penguin Group (USA) Inc., 375 Hudson Street, New York, New York 10014.

To my wife, Leigh, and my daughters, Kate and Ali.

Thank you for your love, your support, and especially your patience during

all the time that I spent putting this book together!

share**retweet**repeat**share**retweet
repeat**shareretweet**repeat**share**
etweetrepeat**share**retweet**repeat**

CONTENTS

Acknowledgments	ix
Introduction	xi

PART ONE

The Big Picture — 1

1	The Fierce Urgency of Going Viral	3
2	Setting Your Goals	16

PART TWO

The Viral Tools You'll Need — 21

3	Building Your Website	23
4	Setting Up Your Email System	45
5	Using Facebook	54
6	Using Twitter	69
7	Setting Up a Blog	81

PART THREE

Crafting Viral Messages — 87

8	Making Your Messages Spread-Worthy	89
9	Using Humor	98
10	Giving Them a Problem	108
11	Using Sex Appeal	116
12	Testing Your Message for Effectiveness	122

PART FOUR

Engaging the Right Messengers   129

  13 Finding the Multipliers   131

  14 Skewing Your Strategy to Multipliers   140

PART FIVE

Jump-Starting Your Effort   145

  15 Advertising   147

  16 Using Google AdWords   159

  17 Advertising on Blogs   164

  18 Facebook Advertising   171

  19 "Echo Echo": Critical Mass Advertising   184

  20 PR: Getting Reporters to Share Your Story   190

  21 Overcoming the "Joy Sponges"   202

  22 Putting It All Together   208

Endnotes   211

Index   213

ACKNOWLEDGMENTS

First, I'd like to acknowledge you, the reader, for actually reading these acknowledgments.

Most folks just skip this section, but you've gone above and beyond because you actually care about all the people who helped make this book possible. That makes you a good person. It also would make you feel pretty guilty if you stopped reading now, right?

Next, I'd like to thank my parents, George and Camille Hlinko, and my brother and sister, George Hlinko and Elizabeth Margulies. Throughout the years, they've been incredibly supportive and always encouraged my attempts to stay on the creative cutting edge (even when those attempts didn't quite succeed).

I'd also like to thank my wife, Leigh Stringer, and our daughters, Kate and Ali. Yes, they've already been thanked in the dedication, but they deserve a second thanks for being my "housemates" as well and enduring firsthand the trials and tribulations of a writer at work. Thanks also to Leigh's parents, Jim and Mary Helen Stringer, both for being the best in-laws a guy could ask for and for always being there to help us out during this process, when the writing made things particularly frenetic.

On the professional front, this book would have never happened without the help and support of my agent, Lauren Abramo, and her firm, Dystel & Goderich. Calling Lauren an "agent" in fact dramatically minimizes her role. Her help with strategizing, brainstorming, and fleshing out the initial idea was crucial. Ditto with my phenomenal editor, Maria Gagliano, and the team at Prentice Hall Press. Maria's work has made this a far, far better book than it would have been otherwise. If you ever end up writing a book yourself, you should be lucky enough to have partners in the effort who are as top-notch as Lauren and Maria.

Thank you also to the millions of grassroots supporters who have backed my efforts over the years and proven that these techniques really can spur revolutions. Without your work and commitment, this book would never have gotten off the ground.

Thank you to everyone else out there who has shown firsthand what the "little guy" can do with the newfound power of the Internet. Everyone from the couple who launched MoveOn.org and redefined grassroots activism (hi, Wes and Joan!) to the kid who started one of the hottest companies on Earth, right from his dorm room (Mark Zuckerberg, I'm looking at you, and yes, I'm very jealous).

Finally, thank you to the people who I hope will be inspired by this book and create some revolutions of their own. The past is a memory, the present is a blur, but you are creating the future.

Let's get started.

INTRODUCTION

Why do some online messages spread like wildfire, while others fall flat? Why do some people spread those messages far more effectively than others? And how can you combine the ideal messages and messengers to make *your messages* explode into ubiquity?

This book will show you how to craft, combine, and implement the components of a truly explosive viral campaign—even if you are working with a tiny budget, or no budget at all.

For most of the last twenty years, I have been knee-deep in the world of viral marketing, moving back and forth between public relations, advertising, comedy writing, technology, and political campaigns. This has included helping lead MoveOn.org, one of the first truly hyper-viral online campaigns, during its initial launch in 1998. It has also including helping lead the highly viral (and successful) DraftObama.org, an effort to build support for then Senator Obama prior to his entrance into the race. Finally, I've been fortunate enough to have worked extensively with a range of Fortune 500 companies, spanning from Walmart to Microsoft to Disney.

Some of the most successful viral efforts I worked on started not with huge companies or organizations, but with small groups or even a single individual. Seeing the way that they too were able to harness the power of viral marketing for incredible success taught me a valuable lesson: *If you are an individual seeking to get your message out to the world, you now have the opportunity*

*to do so in a way that was simply impossible a few decades or even
a few years ago.*

Throughout these efforts, the common thread of my work has been using online technology to build movements and spur buzz—and to do it as quickly and cost-effectively as possible.

This has meant focusing on three key components that I like to call the Viral Trifecta: (1) crafting content that is "spread-worthy"; (2) identifying and engaging the people most likely to spread it; and (3) taking advantage of the technologies that lend themselves most effectively to spreading that content.

Often, when my work has been covered in the media, it's been the technology that got the most attention, if not the sole attention. It's understandable, since that's the most obvious differentiator from the marketing efforts of the past, and frankly where the spotlight is shining most brightly. Let's face it, cutting-edge technology is pretty sexy. It's a huge part of what makes viral marketing even possible. But iTunes wouldn't have listeners without the music, YouTube wouldn't have viewers without the videos, and Amazon wouldn't have readers without the books. Great viral campaigns may spread via cutting-edge technology platforms, but they are ultimately fueled by *spread-worthy content*.

Further, the content doesn't spread itself—people do. Great content in the hands of the right people—what we'll call "multipliers"—has always been the not-so-secret recipe for getting a message to spread ever since people started coming up with messages in the first place.

There is no doubt, however, that new technologies have dramatically increased the potential rewards for a successful viral effort. In the last few years, there has been a profound leap in the *ability* of multipliers to multiply. The emergence of the Internet—and especially social media—has given these individuals the power to quickly spread a message to thousands of friends and family members with a few keystrokes. They aren't just message recipients, they're micro publishers.

This is a profound shift. Never before in human history have so many people had the ability to spread a message so far, so wide, and so quickly. If you are trying to spread a message yourself, understanding this shift and how to exploit it is critical to maximizing your success.

And there's another reason to exploit that shift. We're in a time when consumers are more cynical than ever about the information they receive—especially from companies. According to a survey by Yankelovich, a research firm with a particular expertise in consumer attitudes, 76 percent of consumers don't believe companies tell the truth in advertisements. Their friends, on the other hand, they do still trust (at least, more so than the companies).

If you want your message to penetrate beyond the 24 percent who are still blissfully receptive to advertising, a peer-to-peer spreading component is critical.

We're in a new era, an era where small companies and even individuals can harness the power of viral marketing to compete effectively with the biggest of the big boys. If you learn the rules, and understand the tools, the sky truly is the limit.

PART ONE

THE BIG PICTURE

Why should you care about getting your message read and spread? And why does it matter now?

This section will provide an overview of why viral marketing is suddenly far more important than even a few years ago, and it will describe the elements that make up the Viral Trifecta that is so critical to your success.

Finally, it will show you how to get started by first setting the goals and milestones that will guide your effort and help keep you on the road to your desired destination.

O N E

The Fierce Urgency of Going Viral

How many emails do you have in your address book? Hundreds? Thousands? More? Are you on Facebook? Twitter? How many hundreds or thousands more friends and followers do you have on those platforms?

The simple yet awesome truth is that the typical Internet user can now reach more people with a few keystrokes than Paul Revere reached during his entire ride. And he spurred a revolution.

Got three hundred email contacts? Send ten "cc all" emails a day, and you'll make a million connections in just a year. Got Facebook friends and Twitter followers? For them, you don't even need to "cc all," since your actions are automatically fed into their feeds. "Telling friends" simply happens with each and every update. Thus, these social media platforms are even more important than email for spreading a message. And the power of those using them is growing.

Already, after just a few years, the average Facebook user has 130 Facebook friends.[1] The average Twitter user has 126 followers.[2] And these are numbers for the *average* users. When you look at the top few percent of Facebook and Twitter *power* users, the numbers are far higher. When you get to the real tippy top, the numbers are rather mind blowing.

Singer Rihanna's Facebook page has tens of millions of fans. Yes, she's hugely popular with or without Facebook, but she has the ability to reach tens of millions of people with a few keystrokes. Ditto with Lady Gaga, Eminem, and several others. Think about that. That's something that the Beatles or Elvis never had.

On the political front, Barack Obama has more than twenty million Facebook fans. Sarah Palin has topped three million, and several other presidential aspirants are over a million. Again, with a few keystrokes, they can all reach more people than they could with all but the top national TV news programs.

Think NPR appeals to a narrow audience? Don't tell that to NPR commentator Scott Simon, who long ago passed the one million mark in Twitter followers.

It's not just the mega-famous who are reaching these numbers. In 2011, tech executive Wael Ghonim launched a page on Facebook called "We Are All Khaled Said" (a young Egyptian man who was killed by police) that quickly grew to hundreds of thousands of fans and helped fuel the historic revolution in Egypt. Justin Halpern, a young man living with his elderly dad, put up a Twitter feed that was nothing more than funny quips that his father came up with. "ShitMyDadSays" now has more than two million followers and even spawned a TV show. I myself have started several Facebook pages that engaged hundreds of thousands of fans with almost no marketing budget. One page, "Not Having George Bush as President," managed to gain over half a million fans based on nothing more than a very focused message—aimed specifically at Democratic activists—and a title twist that took advantage of the Facebook feed, that is, giving people the ability to have something show up in their feeds that was rather amusing: "John Hlinko just became a fan of *not* having George Bush as president."

Not every page or email or tweet gets seen by millions of people—*but some do.* And in the age of friction-free spreading enabled by the Internet, every message now has the *potential* to do so.

What the Gutenberg printing press did for books, the Internet has done for "buzz." It has dramatically reduced the cost necessary to get a compelling message out to a mass audience. Never before in human history have so many people been able to spread a message so wide, so quickly.

This is a huge shift, and one that has accelerated rapidly in recent years. Yes, the Internet has been a big deal since the mid '90s. However, in the last few years, not only has there been a continuing increase in the *number* of people online, but there has also been an even bigger increase in the *intensity* of usage. The average American now spends sixty-eight hours per month online,[3] far more time than a decade ago, or even a few years ago. And increasingly, that time is being spent in the hyper-viral world of social media—that is, platforms such as Facebook and Twitter that allow for interactions between users and, thus, accelerate spreading. From August 2009 to August 2010, there was a 43 percent increase in the proportion of time online that Americans spent specifically on social networks (from 15.3 percent to 22.7 percent).[4]

And yet, too many people still create messages like it's the old days. They craft messages to be read, rather than *read and spread.* To a large extent, it's as if we're in the early days of movies, when the first films were nothing more than cameras aimed at a stage, capturing a performance. Too many have not learned to shift their storytelling methods, taking into account the new tools at their disposal. They haven't taken into account the fact that every recipient of information is now also a publisher. One with dozens, hundreds, or thousands of readers at their disposal, and one who can easily spread a message to these readers, if they deem the content to be spread-worthy.

Never before have the rewards been so great for hitting the Viral Trifecta.

THE SINGLE BIGGEST MYTH ABOUT VIRAL MARKETING

If you've been alive and not living under a rock for the last few years, you already know the power of viral marketing. Some examples are just plain fun—millions of views for a video of a baby dancing to a Beyoncé song, for a squirrel on a water ski, or for a particularly embarrassing *Star Wars* reenactment. Some examples, however, are quite profound, such as the idea a kid had in his dorm room that grew via viral spreading into the multibillion-dollar company known as Facebook.

And yet, many individuals who'd love to take advantage of viral power are held back because they believe a myth—the myth that you can't really plan a viral campaign—that they "just happen" if you're lucky. It's a seductive myth, since it gives people license to avoid hard work and analysis, and instead just "shoot from the hip" and hope for the best. But this is about as logical as saying that hit songs are a matter of luck, so we should fire all the musicians and instead just have monkeys slam out a series of random notes to craft a song. Or pretending radio, MTV, and iTunes don't exist, and just expecting the song to spread magically.

Yes, viral spreading takes luck. But there are most certainly steps that you can take to increase your chances of getting lucky. Those steps are encapsulated in the Viral Trifecta.

THE VIRAL TRIFECTA: MESSAGE, MESSENGER, AND MECHANISM FOR DELIVERY

No plan can guarantee you that you will hit a viral home run every time. But you can dramatically increase your chances by focusing on *all three* components of Viral Trifecta:

1. **MESSAGE:** How can you craft content that is not just read but *spread*? What exactly makes content spread-worthy?

2. **MESSENGER:** How can you find the multipliers who will spread your message?

3. **MECHANISM FOR DELIVERY:** How can you take advantage of the highly viral nature of the Internet and social media for spreading your content?

This is an important lesson not just for the marketing, PR, or advertising professional, but for anyone seeking to get a message out effectively and with maximum return on investment: entrepreneurs, musicians, politicians, authors, and even just regular individuals seeking to promote their personal brand. Anyone who wants to understand how to stand out, how to be noticed, and how to get their messages *read and spread* is someone who needs to understand the components of the Viral Trifecta.

Message: Crafting Spread-Worthy Content

Even in the age of the Internet, content is still king. It is the message that is the virus, and ultimately, outstanding content is what fuels virality.

But the definition of "outstanding" changes when your goal moves from getting a message read to getting it spread. A message that speaks to the head is fine, if you want it read. But one that speaks to the heart too is more likely to be read *and spread*. As is one that provokes emotion, uses humor, or in some other way makes the recipient think it is worth *putting their reputation on the line* to spread.

Messenger: Finding Your Multipliers

Nearly everyone *can* spread a message, but only a certain subset of the population—the *multipliers*—actually *does* it, and does it effectively. They may have a larger audience, more credibility, a greater willingness to be overt about their opinions and actions—or a combination of all of these.

Multipliers are the people who will do your work for you. They will spread your message, as long as you give them messages that are spread-worthy—that is, messages that are interesting and that make them look cool, savvy, or in the know. It really is that simple. Multipliers want to multiply things. And in a highly wired, social world, they have the ability to do so at a pace far greater than ever before. But you need to give them a reason.

Mechanism: Leveraging Highly Viral Technology Platforms

We will focus on the Internet and social media in particular as content delivery mechanisms, not just because of their size, but because of their inherently viral nature.

In the world of networks, "Metcalfe's Law" has been a great way of demonstrating the power of a network. Attributed to Robert Metcalfe, an electrical engineer who co-invented Ethernet, it states that the value of a network is proportionate to the square of the number of connected users in the system.

In plain English, an example often used to demonstrate this law is that of the telephone. A single telephone is rather useless. If no one else has a phone, who are you going to call?*

Two telephones would be nice, since you can at least talk with each other. But when you get to ten, one hundred, thousands, or millions, the value increases exponentially.

The same holds true with the viral power of a network. The bigger it is, the more viral it is. If Facebook had a few thousand users, that would be nice, but the virus could only spread so far. But five hundred million? More than half of American adults? Well, that's the difference between a virus that is .00001 percent contagious, and 50 percent contagious—the latter is going to spread a heck of a lot faster and farther than the former.

The same holds true for an individual. The more people in

---

* Not even the Ghostbusters.

their network—Facebook friends, Twitter followers, and email contacts—the greater their power to viralize a message. Someone with two hundred connections, I would argue, is more than twice as valuable as someone with one hundred, given that truly viral messages spread exponentially. Thus, the bigger the initial base of infection, the wider the circle ultimately "infected."

Putting it more simply, as networks have developed more and more connected users, and as users have developed more connections within those networks, the value of individuals as spreaders has increased exponentially.

Okay, now let's move from theory to fact. Consider the following statistics: Facebook has more than five hundred million users. That's nearly 10 percent of *Earth*. Twitter has over two hundred million accounts.[5] While Facebook and Twitter might be getting the most buzz right now, at least in America, they are just the tip of the iceberg when it comes to wildly popular social media platforms. LinkedIn has over one hundred million members. Badoo, another social network, may be virtually unknown in America but has nearly one hundred million members (primarily in Europe). And remember Friendster? It's still got ninety million members and remains popular in Southeast Asia.[6]

Bottom line, not only are these new networks incredibly viral by their very nature, they are absolutely *enormous*. Many seeking to market a message shy away from them, believing them still to be fringe in nature, or restricted to just the young or the early adopters. This is simply not true. Regardless of the target audience you are seeking to reach, the odds are overwhelming that your message will find them in large numbers within social networks. And when that message does find them, they will be in a setting that is incredibly conducive to spreading that message on to others.

Social Networks: The Awesome Power of Peer Pressure

There's another reason why social networks are key. People base their perceptions of reality on the perceptions of those around them. If your friends or colleagues believe something, you're more likely to believe it as well. Sometimes, the power of peer pressure can be truly mind-blowing.

In one particularly fascinating example, the Asch conformity experiments, psychologist Solomon Asch showed just how far peer pressure could go.[7] He asked individuals a series of relatively easy questions, including which line in the right-hand picture, A, B, or C, was the same size as the line in the picture on the left:

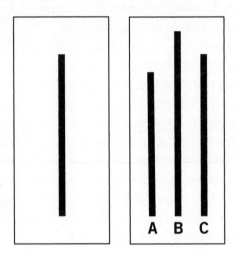

Pretty easy, huh? And indeed, when they were answering on their own, the vast majority, more than 97 percent of test takers, correctly answered "C."

Things changed, however, when Asch put them in a group. A group which, unbeknownst to the test taker, was actually filled with confederates of Asch charged with *deliberately giving the wrong answer, doing it out loud, and doing it before the test taker could answer.* In this situation, the percent of test takers giving the wrong answer rose from less than 3 percent to between 35 percent and 75 percent in different trials.

Think about that. The percentage of people answering incorrectly—and incorrectly in an astonishingly blatant way—went up more than tenfold. *Peer pressure works.* It works really, really well.

Social media platforms, where the opinions of peers are front, center, and in the spotlight, are tailor-made for exploiting the power of peer pressure. When something is shared, it doesn't just inform, it influences.

THE VIRAL TRIFECTA AT WORK: ELECTING A PRESIDENT

Want an example of the Viral Trifecta in action? Look no further than the 2008 American presidential election.

It was early 2008, and the Democratic primary season was captivating the nation. Senator Barack Obama of Illinois had pulled off a stunning victory in the Iowa caucuses, the first contest of the primary season, and appeared poised to capitalize on that victory to sail to the nomination. Just as quickly, however, Senator Hillary Clinton of New York, previously the presumptive front-runner, regained her momentum in a big way with a victory in the New Hampshire primary. A slim victory, to be sure, but one that appeared to establish her once again as the front-runner.

The Obama campaign was thrown for a loop. Had Iowa been a fluke? Was Hillary's famous war machine simply too much to overcome after all? And what about the all-important Democratic grassroots? The committed Democrats who turned out in primary elections, and equally important, helped drive the narrative via blogs and other online chatter? Though Obama's grassroots dominance might seem inevitable in hindsight, it was anything but at the time. Furious debates dominated the Democratic blogs, with many calling to unite behind Clinton as the "inevitable" nominee. Others argued passionately that the (then) highly popular John Edwards was in fact the logical alternative to Clinton.

The narrative had shifted in a big way. The Clinton campaign was once again surging. And with a torrent of primaries coming in the next few weeks, the Obama campaign needed something to shift the momentum—and shift it quickly.

Enter will.i.am, one of the lead singers of the pop group the

Black Eyed Peas. Inspired by a speech given by Obama following the New Hampshire primary, and feeling that an opportunity to make history might be slipping away, Will gathered together a group of celebrity friends and recorded a video—"Yes We Can"—juxtaposing their singing with Obama's speech.

The video itself was quite sparse, shot in black and white, and comprised entirely of straight-on shots of the singers and clips of Obama. As Will himself would tell me later, the process was nothing like that of filming a video for the Black Eyed Peas. Whereas a video for the band might take months, this one was filmed, edited, and released in two days. And whereas the budget for the Black Eyed Peas video might easily be in the hundreds of thousands if not higher, the budget for this consisted of a few thousand dollars for rental of the studio.

In spite of the limited budget and lightning-fast turnaround, this video may have shifted the results of the 2008 presidential election.

Will released the song on February 2, 2008, posting it on YouTube and Dipdive.com. Within three weeks, it had been viewed over twenty-two million times.[8] More important than the quantity of the views, however, was the quality of the *viewers*. It wasn't just a random cross section of Internet users; it was highly concentrated among the Democratic base, and in particular among the "netroots," that is, those grassroots activists using the Internet to drive their political efforts. Markos Moulitsas Zuniga, founder of *Daily Kos*, the largest Democratic blog, began posting the video multiple times a day (each time there was an open thread for discussion). The ripple effect was unmistakable, as other bloggers began doing the same, and the video spread like wildfire among Facebook groups, Listservs, and all kinds of other online gathering places for the Democratic faithful.

To say the video struck a "chord" would be an understatement. In one fell swoop, it served to deliver Obama's core message—hope—in a way that was unbelievably novel, emotionally impactful, and resonant in a way that a straight-on political speech really couldn't be. Even those who might have been cynical about Obama for any number of reasons had a hard time maintaining that cynicism while tapping their feet to the music, and marveling over the fascinating way the video juxtaposed Obama and the celebrities.

The message was delivered in an eminently spread-worthy way.

And the messengers responded. The video did something that even the campaign itself had not been able to. It gave the Democratic netroots, the highly wired activists who lived, breathed, and pontificated online, a way to evangelize for Obama that they were not just willing to spread, but *eager*. It was cool, and made them look cool by association. There were many who might've flinched at the idea of forwarding a standard speech or press release or campaign email to all their friends. But they didn't bat an eyelash at spreading this video, since they knew it would enhance their reputation among those who received it.

And the mechanisms for delivery—YouTube, blogs, email, and social media—were developed enough in 2008 to facilitate this in a way they weren't in earlier elections. It may be hard to believe, but in the previous presidential contest, in 2004, YouTube didn't exist. And Facebook? It was still just a dorm-room startup, mainly a tool for Mark Zuckerberg to try to pick up women.

You already know the rest of story, of course. Obama went on to score a string of victories in the subsequent few weeks. And while Clinton remained in the campaign, by the time early March rolled around, Obama had pretty much established himself as the overwhelming favorite.

Will managed to do all this for a few thousand dollars and a little help from his friends. No marketing budget. No Super Bowl ads. Not one CD or album printed. And yet, with the compelling message and the right messengers, he managed to achieve virality that surpassed that of anything produced by the Obama campaign itself.

The Video Hit the Viral Trifecta

Okay, I hear what you're thinking:

"Sure, will.i.am was able to generate twenty million views. But he's also a lead singer of one of the most popular bands in the country. And he had a gaggle of famous friends to leverage. Is this really an example of the power of the Internet, or just the power of celebrity?"

No doubt there's truth to that. However, it's also true that this was just one of many, many celebrity videos produced during the campaign. And yet, none were even close to it, in terms of virality.

Let's ponder some of the other videos that exploded virally in the 2008 campaign. The Obama campaign spent literally hundreds of millions of dollars on TV advertising. But out of all the commercials and video content produced on behalf of Obama during that cycle, which ones got the most awareness? Three in particular jump out, and they weren't actually done by the campaign. The first was of course the will.i.am video. But what were the other two?

- **A parody of the iconic Apple "1984" ad, but aimed at Hillary Clinton. In the original Apple ad, an authoritarian figure bellowed out orders from an Orwellian telescreen to a sea of drones, watching helplessly. That is, until a lone rebel ran in, threw a hammer, and smashed the screen. In the 2008 version, the authoritarian figure was replaced by Hillary Clinton. And the rebel wore an Obama shirt.**

- **"Obama Girl," aka Amber Lee Ettinger, a lovely young woman singing the song "Crush on Obama." The video was a montage of scenes, all over-the-top romantic clichés of a young woman pining away for a man. It just happened to be a man running for president.**

These were arguably the three most successful videos during the entire campaign. They each generated tens of millions of views, were catapulted into the mainstream media as news stories, and helped shift momentum toward Obama at critical moments.

While will.i.am was able to leverage his celebrity, the same cannot be said of the other two videos. When I met with Phil de Vellis, producer of the "1984" ad, he told me he had literally created it in his apartment over the course of a few hours (appropriately enough, with an Apple computer). And while Obama Girl (aka Amber Lee Ettinger) had the assistance of BarelyPolitical. com, the producers of the ad, there was neither fame nor fortune behind it—just a great, clever idea. Well, and yes, an astonishingly hot star (you'll learn more about the importance of this in Chapter 11).

None of these videos had any paid marketing budget. But they all hit the Viral Trifecta—killer message, eager multipliers, and delivery through a highly viral platform.

- **If the content had merely been "eh," the videos would not have spread.**

- **If they had not gotten into the hands of willing, eager, savvy multipliers, they would not have spread.**

- **And if it were not for the Internet and social media, the viral highway by which this content traveled, they *could* not have spread.**

The makers of these videos hit the Viral Trifecta and helped change the world.

Want to change the world yourself? Or just make your own personal world better? Read on and learn how.

T W O

Setting Your Goals

Before you get going, you'll need a road map to guide you on your journey. Something with goals and milestones to ensure that you're keeping your eye on the prize and getting the most benefit possible from your work.

This is especially important when it comes to crafting a viral campaign, given that the Internet brings with it a nearly limitless array of potential tools, paths—and distractions. Imagine if you were planning a road trip, say, a two-hour drive to the beach. Then imagine that there were billions of different roads to get there, each with a nearly endless number of incredibly cool roadside attractions. Welcome to the Internet. Set your goals, make a plan, craft a road map, and you'll be far more likely to get where you want to go and avoid the perils of an endless series of detours.

WHERE ARE YOU GOING?

Before you can use a road map, of course, you need to have a firm destination in mind. Sure, aimless joyrides can be fun, but not when your business is at stake, and not when you've got a budget to adhere to.

How should you determine your destination? For that we take a cue from advertising legend, and my old boss, Pacy Markman. Not only was he the head writer on the Coke account at twenty-seven, he also wrote what is considered to be one of the most effective tag lines of all time—"Everything you've always wanted in a beer and less" for Miller Lite. This was the cornerstone of a campaign that drove a massive increase in Miller Lite sales, and was named by *Advertising Age* as the eighth best advertising campaign *in history*.

Markman is frankly a creative genius. The kind of guy who could rattle off a dozen great lines in the course of a minute, all on message (and generally, hysterical as well). So you probably think he just starts riffing at will every time a project begins, right?

Wrong. That kind of creativity—any kind of creativity—needs to be contained within focused confines to be effective. Markman starts every project with the same two questions:

1. **Who do you want to reach?**

2. **What do you want them to do?**

Sounds simple, right? Perhaps. And yet, when it comes to the Internet, it's all too common for even the savviest of marketing professionals to get caught up in the technology rather than the strategy. The toys may be new, the technology may be cutting edge, but the basic goals are the same: you want to reach very specific people, and you want to get them doing something.

Not sure of the answers to these questions? No problem. Start out first with this even simpler one:

- **If you were sitting around the table in six months, drinking champagne and celebrating "victory," what would "victory" look like? What goal or goals would you have achieved?**

Force yourself to think through this, and visualize victory. What does it look like? What has happened? What's different? Get as tangible as possible. If you can assign numbers to the goal, do it (increased sales of 15 percent, five thousand Facebook fans, articles in five newspapers, etc.). Make sure the goal is concrete. Something that you will know whether or not you have achieved.

Whatever you do, avoid vague or nebulous goals like "more awareness" or "greater excitement." If you don't refine it into something tangible at the beginning, you'll never achieve it. In particular, if you're working with a group, vague goals will almost always lead to trouble down the road, since they tend to gloss over disagreements or confusion. Everyone can agree on "more awareness," but unless there's a concrete understanding of what that specifically means, ten decision makers in a room will likely have ten different visions in their heads. And more often than not, when no one pushes for specifics, it's because there's a sense that there might be some disagreement, and that it's better swept under the rug.

Okay, with that in mind, let's revisit Markman's two questions:

1. Who Do You Want to Reach?

Get concrete with this question. What does your target audience look like? What are the demographics (age, gender, location, etc.)? What are their interests?

Build a character that personifies your target. "Susan, age thirty-four, fan of the Beatles, loves humor, lives in the city." Or "Jack, age sixty-two, lives in the country, enjoys hunting, and is a sucker for dogs." If you have actual research, great. Otherwise, use your creativity. The more concrete the individual is, the more likely you are to be able to build a plan that really reaches him or her. You'd be surprised how much this helps later, when you're crafting messages, picking advertising venues, and making a zillion other tactical decisions. Being able to ask yourself, "Would Susan/Jack like this?" can help turn hours of agonizing and wondering into a thirty-second snap answer. It forces you to see everything in the context of how it appeals to your target, rather than instinctively judging it by whether it would appeal to you personally.

For example, if you were placing an ad online, you might want to use an image set in a city if you were targeting Susan, but one set in the country if you were targeting Jack. It's a small thing, but making the ad just a little more relatable to the target could make it at least a little more effective. Plus, if you yourself happened to be from the suburbs, your instinct might be to use an image from that setting—an image that would appeal to *neither* target. Force yourself to always look through the eyes of your target audience and to remember that they are not simply clones of yourself.

By the way, if your answer to this question is "everyone," it's very important you punch yourself in the face. Seriously, there are about seven billion people on Earth. You can't reach "everyone." Even ubiquitous brands like McDonald's and Coke don't reach *everyone*. If you try to reach "everyone," you're going to end up reaching no one.

2. What Do You Want Them to Do?

Again, get really specific here. Do you want them to buy something? Tell their friends about something? Sign up for a newsletter at your website?

Get specific. Map out the steps. If they are buying something, are they doing it in a store or online? If they are recruiting friends, are they doing it via email or via Facebook?

Once you have the "who" and the "what," write it down on a page and keep it in a prominent place to guide you through the process. Post it over your desk. Put it on your office door. Tattoo it on the inside of your eyeballs. Use it as your "fixed star" to keep your focus where it needs to be.

TURNING YOUR GOALS INTO A PLAN

Once you get beyond the initial "who/what" stage, you will want to start fleshing out the specifics of your actual plan. The precise shape and scope of that plan will depend on your budget, your time frame, and the specific goal you have in mind. It will also depend on which of the tactics in the chapters that follow are most applicable to your situation.

Your plan doesn't have to be incredibly granular or detailed. In fact, if it is, it's more likely to be ignored than followed. In my experience, the best plans are ones that involve a simple calendar of activities. Typically, I find it most helpful to set up week-by-week columns (in a Word document, Excel spreadsheet, or Google document), and then include rows for the different campaign elements (PR, advertising, email outreach, Facebook outreach, etc.) and for the specific milestone you're hoping to achieve by that date (for example, number of Facebook fans, number of sales, etc.). Yes, you'll need to go beyond this bare-bones approach as you flesh out different elements of it. But having a good forty-thousand-foot overview for your master plan will help keep you on track and help you keep in synch with other members of your project team, if you have them.

As you add elements and you flesh out your plan, keep asking yourself—for every step—whether it gets you closer to your goal. Ask whether it's something that will reach your target audience and get them to do precisely what it is you want them to do.

There's a whole world of things that *could* go into a viral plan—but it's the goal-focused elements only that *should* go into your plan.

PART TWO

THE VIRAL TOOLS YOU'LL NEED

Before you get moving with your viral campaign, you'll need to have the right tools in place to make that campaign possible: A website, an email system, and a social media presence (Facebook, Twitter, etc.).

This section will give an overview of those tools, with a particular emphasis on the features you should look for when choosing them, and the steps you should take to get them set up.

THREE

Building Your Website

f you want to get information out to the masses, a website is the cheapest and easiest way to make that happen. For most viral marketing campaigns, it will serve as the "home" for the content you're seeking to viralize. Even if that content can spread without a site—a top-ten list email, a video, a funny picture, and so forth—you'll surely want an associated site to take advantage of the interest it spawns. YouTube is littered with wonderful videos that generated millions of views—but had no URL on them to give those viewers a place to go next.

Fortunately, building a site doesn't have to mean months of work or a budget in the stratosphere. What you'll want is not a whizbang flashy site designed to impress, but one that is functional and focused like a laser on your goals and needs. This means honing in on the basics, rather than being distracted by all that is possible. It also means striving to make the site as "share-friendly" as possible, something often overlooked by those less attuned to the power of viral spreading. Finally, it means figuring out how you can use the data generated by your site to learn from your users and to hone and refine your campaign moving forward. Let's take it step by step.

BEFORE YOU START MOVING, DETERMINE WHERE YOU WANT TO GO

One of my old colleagues had a wonderful quote about building sites: "The best websites are 80 percent 'built' before a line of code is written." It was the twenty-first-century version of "measure twice, cut once."

Because websites can take nearly any shape, form, and size, it's all too easy to get distracted by all the things you *could* do, as opposed to all the things you *should* do. "Three-dimensional spinning holograms? Sign me up! Replicating the site in ninety-seven languages, including ones that have been dead for three thousand years? Why not! We can do it!"

Remember, as you move through this process, stay focused on your goals: Who do you want to reach? What do you want them to do?

DETERMINE IF YOU WANT TO HIRE A CONSULTANT

If you have the budget, and aren't particularly expert or interested in the nuts and bolts of building the site, or if your time can be spent much more productively doing something else, you might want to hire a consultant. Many people fall prey to the notion that they must somehow do everything themselves, and that it's a badge of honor to really get in the weeds and plod away with coding, design, and content. But there's no sense in spending weeks doing something that someone else could do in hours—especially if it takes you away from something you're better at and where you can add far more value to your overall effort.

Consultants are typically hired for one or more of the following tasks:

- Managing the entire website-building process, from start to finish

- Choosing a platform—the system upon which the website is built

- Coming up with the design—the look and feel for the site

- Determining the information architecture—what goes where on the pages, and how the pages are ordered (this is often included as part of design)

- Developing content—coming up with the words that go on the pages

- Literally, building the site—typing the keystrokes that make it all come together

Don't feel that you *have* to hire a consultant. There are literally billions of websites out there, and the vast, vast majority were built by relative novices. Further, the new tools discussed later in this chapter make the process much easier than in the past. But if you want to go the consultant route, here are your best options for finding one:

- Use personal references. Reach out to family, friends, and colleagues—including your Facebook, Twitter, and other networks. The odds are that at least a few of people will have good recommendations for you. If any of them offer themselves as an option, however, make sure to get samples of their work, and vet them critically as you would any consultant. Better to disappoint an unqualified contact right at the start than to put your entire effort at risk because you want to be nice.

- Find sites that you like, and that appear comparable in scope to what you're envisioning, and contact them: Ask them who they used, what they thought about the experience, and whether they'd recommend them. If you get feedback from a dozen or so website owners, the odds are high that you'll find someone who's a good match for your needs.

■ Search Google, Craigslist, and any local online sources you may have in your community: This is more time intensive, and you'll have to dig through a lot of mediocre ones to get to the good ones. But they're there.

Whichever route you go, make sure to get extensive samples of past work before hiring a consultant. In addition to looking for quality, you'll want to look for diversity of work. Make sure they can do different designs and layouts and can build on multiple platforms (see next section). You won't want someone who is a Johnny-one-note and feels the need to squeeze you into their only mold.

CHOOSE YOUR URL (WEBSITE ADDRESS)

Next, decide what you want your website address to be. This is typically referred to as the domain name or URL ("uniform resource locator" for all you tech trivia types), or more simply, the thing that people type in their browsers to reach your site (Google .com for Google, SierraClub.org for Sierra Club, Wesleyan.edu for Wesleyan University, and so on).

While it's possible to piggyback on an existing URL, and have your page hosted as a subpage of that one, I'd strongly suggest getting your own URL. It will cost you $20 or less and make a much better first impression. Visitors are much more likely to take seriously a page with an address of YourPageHere.com than members.aol.com/YourPageHere or Blogger.com/YourPageHere or some other such name that just reeks of "amateur."

The Mechanics of Finding and Registering a Domain Name
When it comes to choosing a domain name the most important thing is that it is *available*, and available in the ".com" version.

Popular one-word names such as television.com, business.com and pizza.com were snapped up in the early days of the web (and often later resold for a small fortune). You can sometimes get lucky by adding two words together (for example, adding a color before the name, such as PurplePizza.com). Even those can be tough, however, and you may need to search multiple variations.

If you don't get lucky with the first, most intuitive option, and you need to check multiple names, I'd suggest using Instant DomainSearch.com. It's got a great interface that allows you to check name after name quite easily, and instantly find out whether it's available. It actually updates in real time as you're typing in letters, telling you whether the ".com," ".org," and ".net" versions are available. Quite helpful if you're trying to quickly test multiple variations.

Make sure the ".com" version is available. It's the most intuitive of the domain name suffixes, and the one that people are used to typing in. If you're running a nonprofit, you may want to use the ".org" as your main address, since that's typically been associated with nonprofit entities. But you'll still want to have the ".com" version, since some portion of your audience will type that in by force of habit, regardless of what you tell them. If someone else owns the ".com" version, your marketing efforts may end up sending traffic their way. Not good if it's a competitor, but even worse if it's something a little less savory. The official White House page, for example, is hosted at WhiteHouse.gov. That is appropriate, since ".gov" is used for government sites. Not so appropriate, however, was WhiteHouse.com, which was snapped up by some enterprising entrepreneur—who turned it into a porn site. It served up quite a rude surprise for countless good citizens who typed it in, hoping for a lesson in civics and the latest news as to what the president was up to. Even if you're using ".org" or another suffix, make sure to get the ".com" version and set it to forward to the actual site. On a similar front, if you're using the ".com" version for your main site, you're probably best off buying the ".org" version as well, and pointing that to the site. It's less critical than owning the .com version, but still worth it as a defensive measure if nothing else.

Some people have gotten creative as of late, choosing domain names with unusual suffixes, such as ".tv" (the country suffix for the islands of Tuvalu, and a natural suffix for a website focused on television). I wouldn't rule this out if you could come up with something with a phenomenal hook. But if you're thinking that Joes PizzaShop.tv is just as good as JoesPizzaShop.com, think again.

For the actual registration of the name, I like using Yahoo!'s registration service (smallbusiness.yahoo.com). It's relatively intuitive, quick, and allows you to easily change the settings for the domain so it will work with whatever platform and hosting option you choose to use later. The precise way this works differs, depending on the platform, but typically it involves changing DNS settings, such name servers. (Don't let this scare you, it just means a quick change so the domain name knows where to "look" for your site when someone types it in.)

GoDaddy.com is another option for registering your domain name. It's a popular one as well, in part because it's a bit cheaper (especially if you're buying multiple names) and in part because they run an enormous number of TV ads using attractive, scantily clad women (see Chapter 11). It's a good option, though the series of "buy this too" offers before you can actually complete your registration can be a bit of a pain.

Make the URL Intuitive

Make your URL intuitive, easy to spell, and easy to remember. If you say it to someone in conversation, they should be able to type it out when they get to their computer, even if it's hours later.

Remember Gazoontite.com, the start-up that sold allergy and asthma products? No? Of course you don't. No one does. It folded in 2000 after raising $30 million from investors the year before. I'm not saying the name was the only reason it folded, but if people couldn't figure out how to spell it, how the heck could they spread it to others?

The name of your business is typically the most logical name to use for your URL, and if it's intuitive to spell, that should do the trick. If you're running Mario's Wine Shop, for example, you'd be fine using MariosWineShop.com. On the other hand, if that same Mario had used his last name for the shop, and it was something like Pasquadibisceglie's Wine Shop, well, then it might be time to seek out an alternative. Perhaps playing off a specific niche, with something like AwesomeItalianWines.com or BestRedsEver.com.

Don't Be Afraid to Get Creative, Punny, and Memorable

Making it easy to spell and intuitive doesn't mean making it boring. Quite the opposite—use something that will be memorable, funny, and create some cognitive dissonance. Something that will make them stop and say, "Huh?" (critical for standing out in a cacophonous world).

PerezHilton.com, for example, was a playful spin on the name "Paris Hilton" by the blog's founder, Mario Lavandeira. That name was not only funny, it caused the cognitive dissonance necessary to make it stand out, even just for a few seconds—long enough to get noticed. PerezHilton.com now gets tens of millions of page views a week, enough to make it one of the most trafficked blogs on Earth. The name didn't make it, but it gave it a chance to be noticed. And once people noticed it, they read it, enjoyed it, and yes, they spread it.

CHOOSE YOUR "PLATFORM"

Back in the ancient days of website building—the 1990s—there was pretty much one option for building a website—learning HTML and writing the code character by character. The first website I built, back in 1994, took me about a week, even though it was just a few pages. Fortunately, there are a whole range of options available now, options that make building a site far, far easier, even for a novice. That 1994 website? With today's tools, I could probably build it in less than an hour.

The term "platform" is often used to describe some of these alternatives, as they are literally the thing upon which your website sits. It sounds very lofty and techy, but don't let it scare you. If you can use a keyboard and a mouse, you can figure these out.

There are a number of options, ranging from the most ambitious to the simplest.

Custom-Built, from Scratch

Unless you have a huge budget, and extraordinarily custom needs, this probably makes no sense. A decade ago, this was more common. But now, given how far the easier alternatives have advanced, it's really more relegated to huge sites that combine lots of databases and moving parts and have incredibly specialized requirements. Bottom line, unless you're NORAD or a Fortune 100 company, this is probably a waste of time and resources. (I include this less as a viable option, and more as something to push back on, if a consultant tries to get you to go this route.)

Built from Pieces of an Existing System

With this option, you use and piece together different components or modules of an existing technology. Nice, in that it allows you flexibility, but tougher than the more plug-and-play options that follow.

In this category, I'm personally a big fan of Drupal (Drupal. org) and have used it for my own sites. Drupal is free and open source (that is, the source code is public), with the latter resulting in an enormous community of developers constantly adding new widgets and components. You can see installation instructions at the Drupal site, but in a nutshell, you need to download the software, and then install it on a host site. It's less daunting than it sounds, and the instructions on the site are good (though even the "quick" instructions are over two thousand words!). But frankly, it can still be tricky and a time suck for those who are less technically inclined.

Once you have the software installed, you can add a "theme," basically, a preset design, and the additional components for enhanced functionality.

There are other options for this route as well, with Joomla (Joomla.org) being one of the more widely used ones, and probably the closest to Drupal in terms of functionality and flexibility. Like Drupal, it's also open source and free and requires some work to install.

Bottom line, this route offers lots of options, but not without a fair amount of hassle to get started. In my experience, the folks who do best with this approach are the ones who are a bit more tech savvy (or at least not tech-phobic) or who have someone to help with the tech part. It can be rewarding; it can just take a fair amount of tinkering. On the flip side, however, if you are tech savvy and do go this route, make sure that you're not spending too much time tinkering for the fun of it. Keep your eye on the goal, and remember that every minute you spend on something that is not really adding value means getting to your goal at least a minute later.

All-in-One Back-End Platform

These are platforms that combine website hosting, email, and a back-end database all in one system. Salsa (SalsaLabs.com) is a good example, and one I've used myself with great satisfaction. The plus side for these is that you can get your website, email, and database in one fell swoop. Another option is Convio (Convio .com), a very solid system, geared in particular toward nonprofits.

With these systems you typically don't download software, but rather get a separate account that piggybacks on their overall setup. Your information is still private and segregated from other clients, of course, you just use the same back-end functionality (it's basically the same principle as with a web-based email account system such as Gmail or Hotmail).

Unlike Drupal, however, these systems are proprietary, and hosted by the companies that make them. Thus, you are more dependent on innovations from the companies themselves, as opposed to a much larger open-source community. Further, they come with a price (a few hundred dollars to a few thousand dollars a month, typically priced according to how many database records you have). That being said, if you plan on waging a marketing campaign that makes extensive use of email, form sign-ups, and custom content, and if you anticipate having tens or hundreds of thousands of people in your database, this may be worth it for you.

Blog-Based Platforms

In this category are tools and platforms initially developed for blogging, but which can also be used for full-on sites. WordPress is probably the best choice among this group, and one I've used extensively myself. WordPress offers two options: WordPress. com and WordPress.org. WordPress.com is a blogging platform (a place where you can just sign up for a free account and begin blogging using their web-based software). The downside is that your functionality is limited, and your ability to use templates and widgets is restricted to those that work within that system. And again, it's really focused on facilitating blogging, so you might find those restrictions to be cumbersome if your goal is to launch a website that is not blogging-focused.

If you want some more flexibility, I'd suggest checking out WordPress.org. At that site, you actually download the software itself (for free) and then install it on a server to set up your site. With this option, you'll have more flexibility to add functionality and components.

Like Drupal, WordPress (the software) is an open-source tool, and one that you can add themes and widgets to, to create a full-on, highly functional website. In my experience, WordPress software is a bit easier to install and implement than Drupal. And if you want to make it really easy to set up your WordPress software with a web host, sign up for an account with DreamHost (DreamHost.com). It'll cost you a little bit ($8.95 a month or higher, depending on which additional features you use), but it's well worth it. First, the "one-click" installer will set up WordPress in about one minute, as opposed to you messing around trying to install it on a server. Second, DreamHost includes a range of other features that are quite useful, including email.

If you don't want to go the WordPress route, other even easier options are Blogger (Blogger.com) and TypePad (TypePad.com). With both of those, you just sign up for an account and get started—no installation necessary (similar to the WordPress.com option). Both offer some nice options for customization and enhanced design. Still though, I'd strongly suggest considering WordPress.org software installed onto a web host, since it leads the pack in flexibility, functionality, and the number of developers innovating on its behalf.

Template-Based Systems

Finally, there are some nice template-based systems that are made specifically for website building. They're similar to the blog-based systems above, in that you set up an account and then begin to customize. You get a preset template with some ability to customize images and text, but your customization overall is pretty limited on things like numbers of columns, navigation, and headers. Still though, for a starter website, it's worth considering.

Doodlekit (Doodlekit.com) is a nice option, and the system I used for my consulting site (HlinkoConsulting.com). It will get you up and running more quickly than the blog-based approach, since this one really is made with websites, not blogs, in mind. And some of the pricier plans do have some nice features, like a shopping cart, and some header customization.

Once you've picked an approach and decided which platform to choose, it's time to move on to design, content, and implementation.

DESIGNING YOUR SITE

If you're going to get a consultant to help with just one part of the process, design is the one. There's nothing like bad design to turn off a site visitor. It's the first thing they see, and it sends a powerful signal as to how serious your effort is.

If you do choose to hire a designer, however, make sure to pull out that one-pager you did earlier (listing audience and goals, that is, "who and what"), and get the designer on board with it. You will want to make absolutely clear that the design should be focused on achieving an end, not showing off his or her design skills. Beware the "artiste" who is more interested in making pretty things. You want the artisan who knows how to design something that *works.*

If you don't have the budget to hire a designer, however, don't worry. You still have options. And in fact, very good ones.

For most of the platforms mentioned earlier, you have the option of getting "themes" for your design. These are essentially plug-in designs that can be used over and over again by any number of websites on that platform. Themes typically go beyond just the look and feel and also include sample pages, simple forms, suggested fonts, and more. It's not quite "website in a box," but it's close.

The downside to choosing a theme rather than a custom design is that you will have a website that could look like one, ten, or a hundred other sites. Then again, most site visitors couldn't really give a hoot if your site looks like another site they saw weeks or months ago—as long the design is good.

A simple Google search will yield many sources for themes, but I'd recommend starting with these:

- **WORDPRESS: WordPress.org/extend/themes has well over a thousand different themes for sites using WordPress.org software. You can find many more theme sources via Google, but given that these are free (and frankly, many are quite good), it's a great place to start.**

- **DRUPAL: Drupal.org/project/themes also has over a thousand themes for Drupal. And again, there are some very good (and free) ones there.**

- **BLOGGER AND TYPEPAD: Unfortunately, the number of themes on the Blogger site is much more limited. Google (which owns Blogger) appears to have decided not to invest in more than a** few dozen, which strikes me as an odd choice. TypePad has a bit more in the way of options, though still more limited. So start with Blogger and TypePad if you're going with those setups, but be prepared to search Google for additional sources (and note, the process of using themes not offered by these sites themselves is actually a lot less "plug and play" and typically involves really digging into the code itself).

If you choose to craft any design elements yourself (logo, pictures, icons, etc.), consider searching stock image sources such as iStockphoto.com or Microsoft clip art. You'll be able to get images for free or a few dollars. For a good design program, consider Photoshop if you're at an advanced level, or Snagit (TechSmith.com) if you're at a beginning or moderate level. Of course, if you have your own art and images already, you might want to consider using them instead of clip art. As wonderful as clip art is, it can come across as looking generic. Your own images can give a bit more life to your site and speak more to what you're promoting. If you own a restaurant, for example, scenes of happy customers sitting at your tables are far more appropriate than generic shots of generic people eating at generic tables. If you use your own art, however, make sure the quality is good enough to be worthy of your brand. Don't put up something that's sloppy or will come across as amateurish. The photos of happy customers in your restaurant don't need to be taken by Annie Leibovitz, but they also shouldn't have heads cut off, bad lighting, or other elements that shout out, "We really don't care." Regardless of which approach you take on the design front, remember to keep focused on your goals. Don't let "cool design" become a roadblock for getting and spreading information. Remember, it's not about you showing off your Photoshop skills, it's about giving your visitors information they can read, digest and spread as quickly as possible. I still have nightmares of the early MTV.com site—the one with the uber-hip and insanely intricate logo that took about thirty minutes to download on the dial-up service that was overwhelmingly common at the time.

For a sizable portion of its target audience, the site was basically rendered useless. Designers like to show off their skills, which is only natural, and many customers are blown away by "beautiful" mock-ups and imagery. But that's not the point of a design. *The point of a design is to make it as easy as possible for your target audience to do what it is you want them to do.*

CONTENT

You're honing your design, you're set on your platform, and now it's time for content. The exact text and images you choose will of course depend on what you're doing and what your goals are. But here are some basic elements you should at least consider including.

Home Page

This is the landing page where people first come when they visit the site. Typically, you'll want to have a home page that gives the visitor a quick understanding of what this site is all about and prominent links to the other main pages on the site.

The biggest mistake made by new site builders is putting too much content on their home page. Remember, it's not about cramming everything you have in that space, it's about prioritizing the key things you want your visitor to know and do. Google, for example, is one of the most successful websites (and companies) in history, with a market value measured in hundreds of billions of dollars. And yet, the company's home page has been astonishingly simple, even from the start. A search box, a few links to other pages, and that's it—twenty words in total. Now, you don't need to get that extreme, but "less is more" is a rule that almost always applies.

Let's say you were a poet promoting your first book, and that your specific goal was to sell as many books as possible. As an artist, you may be tempted to express yourself on your home page, putting up a statement of why you wrote the book, the trials and tribulations you went through that motivated you, and maybe even a big picture of yourself looking wistfully into the distance. Great, but will that really sell books? What about a big, prominent "buy the book" link to where they can actually buy it? What about a sample of the most compelling piece of your poetry? What about one- or two-line reviews from people (ideally well known) or news clippings saying how wonderful your work is? Think in terms not of what *you* would find cool but of what would spur your target audience to do what you want them to do.

Let's say you were promoting your restaurant. Again, try to get into the mind-set of your target audience. What would be most likely to get a site viewer to actually make the trek there to enjoy a meal? For starters, the address and directions would be helpful. A sample from the menu, along with a click to the full menu would be a big help as well. If you are set up to make reservations online via OpenTable or some other service, include that on the front page as well. Already, with just these three elements, you've told them where you are, what you serve, and whether you have availability.

If you also have a thriving Facebook page, you might want to include a snippet on your home page with a link to it, and either the raw number of fans (if it's a high number that will impress) or a display of the site visitor's specific friends who like that page. Facebook has code that you can easily cut and paste to make this happen. As we saw from the Asch experiments in Chapter 1, peer pressure is a powerful thing and can influence opinions in a profound way. A restaurant with a nice website is great, but a restaurant with a website displaying "1,000 fans" and images of actual friends of the site visitor is even more compelling.

But remember, the bottom line is to keep it simple!

About Page

This is where people go to learn more about who or what is behind the site. In a few paragraphs, try to explain who the person, company, or organization is. But remember, your goal here is not to provide a neutral, encyclopedic overview—it's to impress visitors and make them want to support you. Further, it's to convince skeptical visitors that you're real, and not a scam. So, yes, put the basics here, but also include things designed to impress—news coverage, endorsements from well-known individuals, and glowing highlights from your background. And don't be afraid to show your personality, if that's what appeals to your target audience. SnorgTees, for example, a company selling snarky, fun T-shirts online, has an About page that is similarly snarky and fun (SnorgTees.com/about).

On LeftAction.com, my site aimed at progressive activists, I use the following text on my About page:

> Welcome to Left Action, a network of over 1,000,000 activists committed to making a difference, fighting for progressive causes, and . . . having some fun while doing it. Not sure where to start? Check out our current actions, find ones you like, and . . . start taking action! Or just sign up for updates by clicking here! Get involved today, become part of this exciting movement, and . . . fight back! And make sure to join our Facebook page, and follow us on Twitter!

In the first sentence, I've established credibility ("over 1,000,000 activists"), explained what they can expect ("fighting for progressive causes"), and also let them know what is different about this activist site versus similar ones ("having some fun while doing it"). Right after that, the text moves quickly into specific links where they can immediately start doing what it is that I want them to do.

After that initial paragraph, I include a bio blurb on the founder (me) with links to articles in the *Washington Post*, the *New York Times*, and other prominent media sources (again, to establish credibility, by quoting sources they already trust, instead of just myself).

Contact

This is where people go to figure out how to find you. If you're running a store or other brick-and-mortar business (that is, some-

thing with a real-world address) where you are trying to lure customers to your physical location, make sure to have the address
and phone number and a map clearly posted. Even if you already
have it on your home page, include it here again, since many
folks will immediately click to the contact page when looking for
directions. A nice trick is to link your address right to Google
Maps, so a site visitor can click on it and then enter their own
address for directions via car, mass transit, or walking.

If you're not a brick-and-mortar business, and solely operate
online, you may not want to include your physical address or
even your email address, but instead use a form that submits to
your email (posting an actual email address on a page often leads
to that email being "scraped" by spammers and to the recipient
being flooded with offers for Viagra, easy credit, and million-
dollar paydays from fictitious Nigerian princes).

News

This page is generally used for displaying glowing hits in the
news, or for news updates from the site itself. Some sites actually
separate this page into "press" (press coverage) and "news" (just
updates from the site). Unless you're getting a ton of press and
making a lot of updates, however, you're best off just combining
the two. If you do get press, remember to prioritize your press
hits by the most impressive. Most sites simply list them in reverse
chronological order, which is frankly silly. It's sort of like saying,
"Gees, I won this Olympic gold medal but I got this 'world's greatest boss' coffee mug more recently, so I guess I should display
that instead." On ActForLove.org, for example, a dating site I run,
the top quotes are from a few years ago—but they're at the top
because they're glowing, and they're from *Newsweek* and the
New York Times.

Beyond that, you'll want to include other pages that are relevant to your goals—driving action, sales, sign-ups, whatever they
might be.

Prioritizing Your Content

Whatever content you choose to put on your website, make sure to prioritize.

You've got five things to say? Great! But there's no rule that says they have to have five equal amounts of space and prominence on your site. Pick the most important thing, and give it the most prominent space. If you have the budget, you may want to bring in a trained information architect at this point, someone who can figure out the optimal placement of information for the user (basically, what will get them to do what you want them to do). If you don't have the budget, then start by looking at comparable sites (in scope, size, and focus) that are successful, and replicate what they do. Don't copy them line for line, but look for common traits, and recognize that there's probably a reason they're so common. For instance, 99 percent of restaurants have a menu on their site for a reason, 99 percent of photographers have sample pictures on their sites for a reason, and 99 percent of (insert your category here) websites prioritize certain content elements for a reason.

Once you have your site set up, remember that it doesn't have to be (and shouldn't be) set in stone. Keep an eye on site traffic reports over time. If you find one page is consistently getting far more views than another, you may want to consider prioritizing its content on the home page. Again, focus first on what it is you actually want visitors to do, as that's the whole point of having a site in the first place. But pay attention to what it is that's engaging them most, what it is they're spreading, and recalibrate accordingly over time.

MAKING YOUR SITE AS "SHARE-FRIENDLY" AS POSSIBLE

Whether you are building a mega-million-dollar site or a shoestring one, there are some general things you'll want to keep in mind above and beyond the basics, if your goal is to make it "share-friendly."

Make Sure Each Page Has a Unique URL That Can Be Cut, Pasted, and Spread

A scarily high number of websites still think it's cool to keep the main URL at the top as people click through from page to page, and mask the address of the specific page the person is on. Nice on paper, but a royal pain if someone sees an interesting page and wants to pass it on.

Unless you've gone out of your way to do it, the odds are slim that this would happen by accident. Most typically this happens when someone sets up a domain name in one place and forwards it to the actual site using what is called a "masked forward" option—that is, deliberately keeping the URL at the top and masking the actual site address below it. If you've registered your domain through Yahoo!, for example, per my earlier recommendation, changing this is a simple matter of clicking "standard forward" instead of "masked forward" in your domain control panel. Other sites should have something similar, if you poke around. If on the other hand your consultant has done this, or recommended doing this, politely tell him or her that you'd prefer to take the "non-stupid option" instead.

Also, make sure the URLs for individual pages are not insanely long. The last thing you'll want is for someone to forward a message via email and have the URL break and become unclickable. Almost all of the platforms described earlier give you the option to set a page URL. Typically, they'll come up with one by default based on the title you give the page, but offer you the option to change it.

Provide Tools That Make It Easy for the Visitor to Spread Your Message

Make sure to install Facebook and Twitter widgets on your site so users can simply click to spread a page automatically (see those sites for installation instructions). The AddThis widget (AddThis .com) also lets users share across a range of social/bookmarking platforms.

The process for installing widgets varies depending on how your website is built, but it is typically pretty straightforward. Add-This, for example, simply requires you to add a few lines of code, something that would take a fairly savvy techie about five minutes, and even a novice less than an hour. Once you have done this, each one of your posts and pages will automatically include a small box with icons from several different platforms (Facebook, Twitter, etc.). A simple click is all that the viewer will need to do to share. It sounds like a small thing, but reducing sharing from a process that takes a few minutes of cutting and pasting to one that takes a few seconds and one click is a big deal. Getting people to spread a message for you is often less about convincing them to do it and more about making it easier to do it *for the ones who already want to.*

COLLECTING DATA

The beauty of the Internet is that every action creates a piece of data to go with it. The data that you collect via your website will be critical in helping you refine your effort over time, improve your response rate, and maximize the spreading of your content.

The extent to which you can collect data, and the type of data you can collect, will vary depending on the platform you choose. At a minimum, however, most of the approaches described earlier will give you basic stats, such as page views. That's a good start, but you'll want to track more. There are a range of plug-ins and services for doing this, but frankly, when it comes to "tracking more," it's hard to find a better friend than Google Analytics.

Google Analytics (Google.com/analytics) is a wonderful tool for getting more data out of your site. Installing it is a fairly simple process, usually involving just inserting a few lines of code. For some platforms, there's already a plug-in, making it even easier. Google gives instructions for installation on the Analytics page. For most sites, it should take no more than a few minutes.

Once you have Google Analytics installed, you'll be able to track a tremendous amount of data relating to your site, including:

- **VISITS:** Including number of visits, unique visits, average time on site, total page views, percent who viewed more than one page, and percent new

- **SOURCES:** What sites your traffic came from, what keywords people used to find you, and which search engines sent them

- **CONTENT:** Including how many views each individual page had, top landing pages, top exit pages, and so on

There's more, but this should give you the idea. Beyond that, you also have the ability to examine each of these stats within a date range that you specify. If you're interested in getting really advanced, Google Analytics also allows you to set up custom "Goals" to measure a specific path. For example, what percent of visitors to your home page actually completed a sign-up, or what percentage of visitors to a product page end up actually buying the product. Finally, it allows you to set up custom reports, measuring things such as how your traffic sources differ in different countries.

Did I mention that it's also free?

Unless your website platform already has all this data, you should absolutely install Google Analytics.

GETTING PERSONAL

Where Google Analytics falls a little short, however, is in tying specific pieces of data to specific individuals. It may tell you that you had 818 visitors to a page—but it won't tell you who those 818 people were. It may tell you that 21 percent of those visitors are repeat visitors—but won't tell you which are which. And it may tell you that a link in an email generated 917 clicks, but it won't tell you who clicked.

If you want to get really personal with your data and track people at this level, and you have the budget, your best bet is to go with one of the "all-in-one" back-end systems described above— one of the ones that ties page hosting, email, and database into one package, such as Salsa (SalsaLabs.com). Once someone signs up on your site, typically through a form of some sort, it syncs up further activities into one unified record. Thus, if "John Hlinko" signs up on your site, he is instantly put into your database. When you send an email to that database, the system automatically tracks which one went to John Hlinko. If John Hlinko clicks on a link in that email, that goes into his record. And finally, when John Hlinko visits the site again, you can customize it to welcome him.

When email, web, and database systems are separate, however, syncing up this data becomes more of a challenge. Basically, you'll need a technical solution to bridge the systems so that data can flow back and forth in real time, and the systems can respond to that data. If you've got a lot of technical expertise at your disposal, you could try diving into the world of coding and giving this a shot. Also, new plug-ins for open-source systems like WordPress are emerging all the time, so it couldn't hurt to do some searching when you're ready to begin. If it becomes apparent, however, that this is going to lead to a massive time suck, you may want to think twice.

STOP HYPERVENTILATING, JUST TAKE YOUR BEST SHOT

If this seems a bit daunting, don't let it "daunt" you. Remember, your first website doesn't have to be your last, and you can always make gradual changes over time. You don't need to incorporate every feature described here from the beginning.

Focus on the basics, don't be distracted by all you *could* do, and focus instead on what you *should* do. As long as your site is goal-oriented, is designed to help your target audience do what you want them to do, and built to make spreading as easy as possible, you will definitely be on the right track.

FOUR

Setting Up Your Email System

When it comes to online communication, email is still the "killer app," the tool we'd probably freak out most about if we had to give it up. The average person may visit their favorite sites a few times a week, if that. Even with Facebook, the ultimate sticky site, only half of its users log on more than once a day.

But email? Most users check their email multiple times per day—if not per minute. In fact, in an age of iPhones and Black-Berrys, the nearly constant tether that so many have to email makes it more important than ever. No doubt, you'll hear lots and lots of reports about the death of email, and its replacement via texting, social media, or some other new technology. And you'll invariably receive and read those reports—via email.

Even if you have legions of Facebook fans or Twitter followers, and even if your efforts on those platforms are thriving, you'll still want to entice them to give you their email addresses. Remember, these platforms could disappear or change their terms of service in a way that limits the effectiveness of your communications. It's their platform, and they control it. Facebook is largely controlled by one dude, Mark Zuckerberg. Clearly, he's smart as hell, but who knows, he could wake up one morning having a bad hair day and decide to remove page updates as a feature. Don't put all your eggs in one basket—especially not if that basket is being held by someone else.

Further, most platforms and tools still use email addresses as the unique identifier. If you want to scan your database to see who's on Twitter, for example, you can't use Facebook screen names, you need to enter email addresses.

WHAT YOU'LL NEED

We'll get more into tips for crafting email messages later, but let's start with the functionality that will enable that content to be delivered most effectively and efficiently. Whatever system you choose, make sure it offers these features.

Easy Importing of New Members

Make sure that the email system you choose allows you to easily import your list when you start, as well as future lists you may acquire. Typically, this is done via an Excel spreadsheet or CSV file (basically, a file where the variables are separated by commas. Excel and most comparable programs allow you to "save as" this type). Ditto with *exporting* the file, in case you later want to take your names and use another system.

Ability to Send Email to Subgroups

Depending on what data you have, you may want to do things like email people only in a certain city or of a certain gender or age, and so forth. An email about a concert in New York might not be terribly relevant to a recipient in San Diego. An announcement about a monster truck rally might be more relevant to a twenty-five-year-old male than an eighty-five-year-old female.

You may also want to email people based on performance. People who respond eagerly to every email might merit a very different email from those who respond every few months. You may want to include a more ambitious request for the former, since they appear more engaged. For example, if you were running an activist campaign asking supporters to email Congress, you might ask the frequent responders to go the extra step and make a phone call or even request a meeting with their members. This higher level ask might be off-putting to those only fleetingly engaged, but perfectly appropriate to those more deeply engaged, and perhaps champing at the bit for more.

To differentiate in this way, you'll need a system that tracks user responses over time, allows you to automatically group frequent responders by using queries, such as "opened at least eight emails sent over last two months" or "clicked through at least five times," and then allows you to restrict emails to just that group. If your system doesn't do this, you could do it manually by adding a "Frequent Responder" field, and updating it to "yes" or "no" depending on how the individual has responded to the last few emails (not ideal, but doable if your email list is of a manageable size).

Ability to Customize Email Based on Subscriber Data

The more customized and personalized an email, the better the odds that it's going to get read, spread, and acted upon. However, the last thing you'll want to do is personally write an email for each individual on your list. Your fingers will probably fall off by the time you finish the first thousand.

You'll want a system that can automatically insert different information based on different fields, such as name and location. Ideally it should be able to draw information from a database on the fly, and insert that information into the emails based on the profile of the user. For example, filling in the blank in something like "We're about to launch our new manure-powered convertible, and here are the <<insert number>> places where you can test-drive it in <<insert city>>."

Typically, such systems are set up to allow you to insert codes in an email that are then magically transformed into actual values drawn from a database (example: "#City#").

Automatically Subscribe and (More Important) Unsubscribe

The last thing you'll want to be doing with a list of any size is manually unsubscribing people. Further, easy unsubscribing for the user is critical, lest you become the target of spam complaints and start to have your emails filtered out. Most email programs make it easy for the user to mark an email as "spam." And if your unsubscribe link is buried, and the "spam" button is prominent, you're going to get hit with spam complaints, regardless of whether or not they're valid. Once you start accumulating enough of these, email systems will start to automatically deposit your email in the spam folder by default.

Track Activity on an Individual Basis

If you have a list of ten thousand recipients, and there are three thousand opens of your email, you should be able to track which three thousand recipients specifically opened it. If one thousand of these click a link to go to your site, you should know who those are as well. Fortunately, there are many fine systems out there that can do just that, and can do it without breaking the bank.

If you are using one of the all-in-one platforms mentioned in Chapter 3, such as Salsa or Convio, then your email tool is already taken care of. Both of those systems include the features mentioned here. If, however, you're using one of the other platforms for your site, one which does not include an email tool, you'll need to get a separate one.

I've used MailChimp (MailChimp.com) and Vertical Response (VerticalResponse.com) and would recommend both. They both include the features above, and do a nice job of being user friendly for newbies without being dumbed down for those with more technical proficiency. I'd probably give a slight edge to Mail-Chimp, since its interface is a bit easier for formatting a nicely designed email. But frankly, they are very close, so I'd suggest you play around with both (free trials are available) and see which one feels more comfortable.

Prices for both are roughly comparable, ranging from very cheap or free if you have a few hundred or even a few thousand records (email addresses) in your system, to a few hundred dollars a month if you get more into the tens of thousands of records range. Both also offer different pricing plans, based on whether you want to pay for a longer term in advance, and whether you want to pay per email sent rather than database size. My advice would be to assume that you're going to send two emails a month to your whole list, and choose which option makes sense on the basis of that.

Once you start getting into the tens of thousands of email range and beyond, the price for tools such as these starts to nudge up more and more toward that of the all-in-one systems. Thus, if you are not using an all-in-one platform, and your list starts to hit this range, it may be worth considering switching over to one to take advantage of the other benefits. Note: This is not an easy switch, since it will almost certainly require some rebuilding of pages to conform with the new system, rather than a simple transfer of code.

CRAFTING YOUR EMAIL

Once you have your system ready, it's time to start sending emails. Remember, no matter how good your site is, you can't expect people to keep coming to you—you need to reach out to them. We'll talk in more detail in Chapter 8 about crafting spread-worthy content, but for now, let's start with the best practices for the different elements.

Try to Come up with a Good Frequency
Typically, an email every two to three weeks is a good, reasonable pace. You can get more frequent if you have a really passionate

audience or a temporary need (say, multiple reminders to vote the week before an election). But otherwise, I'd be wary of it.

To optimize your frequency, however, watch how people react over time. If you start seeing a lot of people complaining about the frequency or unsubscribing, you may want to consider emailing less frequently. Ditto if you see the open rate start to decline. On the other hand, if you're getting a very strong response—lots of opens, clicks, and spreading, you might try increasing your pace.

Pick a Good "From" Line

This is literally the "from" that people see when your email arrives—that is, who sent it. You'll want to use something that's descriptive and accurate, but catchy. Avoid things like "info@" or "webmaster@" or other things that sound techy and nonhuman.

Try using names of real people, even if it's in conjunction with the organization name. For example, I use "John Hlinko, Left Action" when I send my emails to the Left Action list, and it seems to work well.

But try a few different ones and see what works best. The differences can be quite profound, and surprising. Back in 2004, I worked on the Wesley Clark for President campaign. Four-star general, very serious candidate, passionate grassroots following, and yet, the "from" line that got the biggest response? "Madonna@." She sent an email on the campaign's behalf, and open rates were off the charts. Another campaigner, working for a Republican candidate, confided to me that while the candidate's name got a decent open rate in the from line, using the names of female staffers actually did better (especially, he admitted, if the names sounded "cute.").

Pick a Good Subject Line

Along with the "from" line, the subject line is the biggest indicator of whether an email gets opened. It should be short (forty characters or less) to avoid getting cut off. It should be provocative, not just blandly informative. And it should leave them wanting more—and wanting to open up the email itself to get that "more" part. For example:

- **What's the world's most popular wine?**

- **Which "green" company pollutes most?**

- **Two-for-one cupcakes at Enzo's bakery**

Catch their attention, and give them a good sense of what they're likely to see or learn about in the email. Don't be too cutesy or sales-y, since that will raise a "cynicism filter" among your recipients.

Further, most email systems allow some degree of automatic customization in the subject line. Entering a name, city, or some other element that personalizes it could catch the recipient's eye a bit more and provoke an open.

Finally, make sure to test your subject lines, since what works for one effort and audience might perform quite differently for another. We'll get into the specifics of testing in Chapter 12.

Craft Compelling Content

The body of the email is what gets read and what gets spread.

In general, a good rule is to write it like a press release (see Chapter 20) with a provocative headline, and three to five hundred words that tell a good story. Further, assuming that you want them to click to go somewhere (say, to your site), include the link a few times. Make it easy for them.

Most systems these days will also allow you to include design. Don't get over the top here, but do try to incorporate a simple background design that matches your site, and an image or two that syncs up with your text. Be careful that your images aren't too big, however, since you don't want to annoy the recipient with a big download. Also, know that some recipients block images or have their setting on "text only," so don't use images that are critical to the email (where the email would make no sense without them).

Finally, ask them to spread the message. I typically include something to the effect of "Please forward this to your ten thousand closest friends!" It's cheeky and silly, but it invariably drives up the pass-along rate.

Text Versus HTML

On the "text only" note, most email systems these days give you the option of sending both, with the system sniffing out automatically whether the recipient should get the html or text version (more or less). This simply means that after you write your html version, you should be able to cut and paste the text (text only, not code) into a text-version area as well.

(It's less complex than it sounds, but just be aware that having some recipients getting text only doesn't mean you need to dumb it down for everyone).

Spam-Filter Testing

Finally, you'll want to make sure your emails don't trigger spam filters, which prevent them from being seen at all.

Nearly all email recipients these days use some kind of mechanism to keep as much spam as possible from landing in their inboxes. Gmail, AOL, Yahoo!, and most of the biggest known email options have filters built in that either autodelete suspected spam or send it to a spam folder that the average person will never check. Other systems, such as Spam Arrest (www.spamarrest.com), can be added on as supplements to an email system to act as a gatekeeper. All of these filters basically work the same way, scanning for things that might indicate that an email is spam, such as certain keywords ("Viagra," "sex," "porn," "free," etc.) or email characteristics (a lot of extra HTML code, for example).

Fortunately, there are ways of testing your email before you send it. More and more systems for sending email include a spam-check as one of the steps before you can launch it. If yours does, make sure to take advantage of it. If not, SpamCheck (http://

spamcheck.sitesell.com) is a nice (and free) service you can use. You can test your email for spamminess by either entering it in a form on the site or by emailing it to spamcheck@sitesell.net (make sure to use the word "test" before the subject line, so it doesn't inadvertently get filtered out). SpamCheck instantly gives you a report with a spam ranking, and details regarding what potential problems (spam triggers) your email might have.

FIVE

Using Facebook

I f you're living on planet Earth, walking upright, and have ever seen a computer, you've probably heard of Facebook. And if you're in the United States and over eighteen, the odds are that you have a Facebook profile yourself.

Facebook is the big player in social media, with over half a billion people using it. This number is astonishing, considering that some kid, Mark Zuckerberg, started it in his dorm room just a few years ago. In fact, Facebook is not only a social media channel, it well might be the single best example there is of a viral marketing success. It was a very compelling idea, its praises were sung via a highly viral platform (its own), and it spread like wildfire. Initially just among the college audience for which it was first intended (not coincidentally, some of the most fervent multipliers there are), but once opened up, to the rest of the world.

FACEBOOK: THE BASICS

Facebook is a platform that lets you easily deliver content to friends, create discussions around that content, and enable these friends to easily spread it to their friends and beyond.

Facebook allows you to do the following:

- **SET UP A PRESENCE:** Individuals set up "profiles," while organizations set up "pages." In both cases, the first step is to put up some basic information to give visitors a quick overview.

- **POST UPDATES:** Want to post a picture? A link to another site? A video? A pithy statement? Go ahead, just type it into your status bar, and it will be posted on your profile or page. Essentially, it functions as a mini-blog.

- **MAKE CONNECTIONS:** Individuals can link to other individuals as "friends," and thus opt in to their updates. When you log in, you'll see their friend updates in a list, aka a "feed," and they'll see yours on their feeds. Organizational "fan" pages are a little different, with the communication going in one way only. If you're the Acme Widget Company, for example, and someone decides to "like" your page (and thus become a fan) that means they will see your status updates in their feeds. But the feed will not go the other way, and their updates will not show up on your page.

That's Facebook in a nutshell. You put your stuff up, and people who've opted in to see your stuff have it show up on their page. And if they like that stuff, they can easily share it with their friends through a simple click. Simple, but also so simply brilliant. All Facebook is really doing is making the spread of compelling content easier and more efficient. They're making it as near to friction free to spread a message as one can get. And that's what makes it so powerful.

GETTING STARTED

If you're not familiar with Facebook, take ten minutes right now to set up an account and play around a bit. You really need to dive into the world of Facebook firsthand to understand this stuff. For everyone else who's at least a little familiar, let's jump into how you can use it to promote a cause, company, product, or yourself.

Your first step is setting up what is commonly referred to as a fan page but which Facebook simply refers to as a page. Again, this is different from a personal profile page. A profile page is wonderful for connecting with friends and family, but a fan page is what you will need to drive your marketing campaign, and that is where we will focus.

Choosing a Name

Before you start building, decide what you want to name your page. Typically, most go with the straightforward route, using a company name, organization name, or a product. However, you can get clever with names as well. For example, Leigh Stringer, author of a book called *The Green Workplace*, a discussion on how companies can make their workplaces more environmentally friendly, set up a page by that name. "The Green Workplace" got over a thousand fans, which is quite nice for a book. She supplemented it, however, with another page called "Supporting Green Companies." That quickly rocketed to fifteen thousand fans. Why? Because the book was a new thing to these people, but "supporting green companies" was something they already knew they liked. Plus, they liked having it show up in their feeds that they were a "fan of supporting green companies." The people who signed up for that page, however, were still eminently logical potential purchasers of the book, so it was a wonderful way of getting them on board for future pitches.

If you can come up with a similarly creative approach, consider it as a page name, even as a supplemental page to your main one. A word of caution, however: Facebook has a habit of disabling what it views as "generic" pages, and the definition seems to change without warning. Thus, early creators of pages such as "pizza" and "music" found their pages disabled, often after garnering hundreds of thousands or even millions of fans. Why Facebook chooses to punish success is something that frankly baffles me, but it is what it is.

Your best bet, if you go the creative route, is to buy the website domain of the same name (for example, SupportingGreen Companies.com) and set up a simple site. This will allow you to claim with a straight face that your page is representing a website, and not a generic page. This approach appears to work with Facebook, or at least it has in my experience.

Two final notes to consider: (1) Facebook will let you change a name if you have fewer than one hundred fans, so don't freak out if you have a typo. But remember, once you get to one hundred, you are stuck with that name. (2) If you're planning on doing advertising for the page, try to keep the name to twenty-five characters or less. We'll get into the weeds of advertising later, but some Facebook ads must use the page name as the ad headline, and the headline cuts off at twenty-five characters (see Chapter 18 for full details).

Building Your Page

Once you're set on a name, you're ready to build your page.

First, log in to Facebook using whatever account you'd like to use to administer the page. It can be your personal account, though in many cases, companies choose to create corporate accounts that can be shared by employees. You can always add other page "admins," people who have the same permissions to edit the page, post updates, and see statistics. But be aware that any admin who is added also has the power to remove other admins (including you) and even to delete the page.

Once you're logged in, look for the link to "Pages" on your home page. Most likely, it'll show up on the left, though you may need to do a little poking around if you don't see it right away (Facebook has a tendency to move things around a lot).

Once you've gotten here, this is what you'll need to do:

1. **Create and categorize your page:** Click "Create a Page," and choose a category for your page. Facebook offers a range of categories, so poke around a bit and try to find the one that matches your page the best. Note: Facebook does allow you to change this later, but I'd still recommend choosing carefully, just in case they decide to nix this option.

2. **Enter information about your page.** At this point, your page should pop up, though it'll look pretty empty. It's time to start fleshing it out. The precise options for what you can fill in will differ slightly, depending on your category, but it will always include an "About" section, where you'll want to fill in a quick blurb about your page. This About blurb will later show up on the "wall" of the page (the tab where people land by default), so think carefully about what would be a good quick hook for first-time visitors to the page. In addition, you'll want to fill in the URL of any associated website, such as your company/organization website or a website specific to that page, if you have one.

3. **Choose a picture.** This will be the image that shows up to represent your page, both on the sidebar and as the icon that appears in others' feeds alongside your status updates. Take a minute and look at your own feed on your personal profile page. Look at the picture icons alongside friend and page posts (that is, the pictures that show up to represent them). Notice how some stand out from the others? Those will get more clicks. Keep this in mind as you choose your picture. Make sure it's crisp, clear, and eye-catching, even at that tiny size. So, no big crowd shots. Think more in terms of what would look great on a postage stamp (and, yes, you can change it later).

That's all it takes to get a fan page set up. Facebook will

advise you with a "getting started" tab on other things to do, but at this point, your page is live.

As a next step, you'll want to get a shorter URL. When you first set up the page, Facebook will give you an impossibly long URL, like "http://facebook.com/pages/This-URL-Sucks-Eggs/10150152034195401." Sure, it's functional, but not terribly memorable nor spreadable. And there's a good chance it will break if forwarded via email. Once you have twenty-five fans (twenty-five people who've clicked "like" on your page), Facebook lets you go to Facebook.com/Username and pick a shorter "vanity" URL. Something like "Facebook.com/SuckEggs." Small thing, but every little thing helps when it comes to making your message more spreadable. This is especially true if you intend to use it offline, in places such as posters, TV ads, or newspaper ads. Also, if you have a specific brand you want to promote, say, Joe's Widgets, you'll want to make sure to claim "Facebook.com/JoesWidgets" before someone else does, whether it happens to be a competitor up to no good or some random dude who coincidentally happens to be named Joe Swidgets and who thinks it'd be neat to have his own name as his vanity URL.

GETTING FAMILIAR WITH YOUR PAGE STATISTICS

Once you have your page set up, get familiar with "Insights," the Facebook statistics for your page.

If you are logged in and are an admin for a page, you should see the "Insights" link when you go to the page. The stats are limited, and nowhere near as robust as Google Analytics, but still good for giving you a view of overall trends—numbers of fans, fans who have left or hidden your posts, interactions per posts, active users, and a number of other indicators of how your page is doing. Keep referring back to these stats to see whether what you are doing is working—increasing the number of fans and interactions—and use to optimize your strategy moving forward.

Note: There is a typically a delay in Insights of a day to a few days, so don't be alarmed if you see lots of zeroes when you first start.

PLANNING YOUR STATUS UPDATES

Now that you have your page up, it's time to start posting status updates. This is the real power of a page—the ability to instantly send messages to fans, to keep them engaged and interested and get them evangelizing for you. We'll talk in more detail in Chapter 8 about crafting spread-worthy content, but for now, let's start with the Facebook basics.

As you craft your status updates, remember that the goal is not just to get things read but to get them spread. This means getting noticed, but it also means spurring interactions among your fans—most typically, sharing the post, making comments on it, and clicking "like" (both on the post itself, and on comments by others). This is what spurs viral spreading. Each time a fan interacts in this way, there is some chance that that action will show up in the feeds of their friends. Facebook is constantly refining its algorithm as to what exactly does show up, but the bottom line, the more interactions you get, the more likely those interactions (and the link to your post) will show up in the feeds of their friends, leading some percentage of those friends to become fans themselves.

Here are some steps you can take to optimize your posts and posting strategy:

Try to Come Up with a Good Pace of Posts

Typically, two or three posts a week is a good rate for most pages. That would be a lot for email, but since posts are less intrusive—showing up when the user chooses to look at his or her feed, as opposed to deposited in their inbox—it's eminently reasonable for posts. Watch your fan interactions over time, in order to really hone in on the optimal pace for your specific page. If you start seeing a lot of people complaining about the number of posts in comments, or if your Insights show that people are "unliking" your page or hiding your posts, you may want to consider slowing down. On the other hand, if you're getting a very strong response—lots of interactions and happy fans—you might try increasing your pace. Remember, each post is a chance for fan interactions, and each fan interaction is a chance to infect someone else's feed and get a new fan.

Get to the "Hook" Quickly
You've now got more than the original 420 character limit to make your point. But try to do it in the first 50 anyway. Remember, they're seeing your update as just one of many on the page. Grab them quickly, or you risk losing them.

Make It Interesting and Provocative
Remember, you want your post to be spread-worthy. Whatever you do, don't put up one that's a yawner, just because you feel the need to post something. Each boring post increases the chances that your fans will either leave or simply stop clicking over when they see your page pop up in their feed.

Make the Content Appropriate for Social Media
This is not just a medium for making announcements or posting press releases, it's one for spurring conversation. Don't come across as stiff and overly PR-ish or, frankly, full of BS. Fans aren't coming to your page for ads packaged as posts, they're coming to interact. Ask them questions. Get their feedback. And don't just talk about yourself; throw out topics from the news for conversation. Make it an interesting place to be and interact, not just a series of bragging points.

Engage with the Fans
Don't just post and run, hang out for a bit and comment back and forth. A lot of fans really are pleasantly surprised when the page owner responds to their comments.

When You Post, Attach a URL, Picture, or Video

This will make it stand out more in fan feeds, by making the post take up a longer amount of space and by adding an image (Facebook automatically includes a still image of the video or an image drawn from the referenced URL).

Pop on to Facebook now and look at your personal feed. Notice how the updates with images attached really stand out and get your attention? In my own experience, a good image can double or even triple the response.

Facebook Marketing Director Randi Zuckerberg (and yes, she's Mark's sister) concurs. As she said in the social media news site *Mashable*, "My #1 tip to businesses who want to grow their Facebook presence requires no additional work—it's simply to include a photo with every post. A picture truly is worth a thousand words."[9]

Ask Fans Directly to Like the Post, and to Share It

There's nothing wrong with being quite blatant about this. You may feel you're going over the top and even veering into cheesiness, but if you ask directly, you will get more interactions. For example:

- Click "like" if you'd like action novels to actually have more action. Then click below to get a sample of my new novel, *Action Reaction.*

- Click "like" if you would like your leaders to do something about the deficit!

- And remember, good news is meant to be shared, so . . . share this post right now!

In my experience, this consistently drives up the number of interactions, often doubling or tripling them versus comparable posts without the ask.

Solicit Comments

Facebook is an interactive medium—take advantage of it! Ask for comments directly and make it easy by giving them something to comment on that doesn't take a lot of thought or expertise. For example:

- **Love New York? Tell us what you love most about it! Leave a comment below!**

- **(with picture) Got a caption for this picture? Give us your best in a comment below, and we'll give a shout-out to the one that gets the most likes!**

These steps should get you off to a good start. But remember, the proof is in the pudding, and the real measure of success for your post and posting strategy will come from the results. Keep an eye on the page Insights and reactions to individual posts, see what works, and keep adjusting accordingly.

MARKETING YOUR FACEBOOK PAGE: WAYS TO GET MORE FANS

People who visit your page will make a judgment about its seriousness in part by the number of fans. If there are only thirty or forty fans, it sends a market signal that it's not a terribly interesting place to hang out and that the entity behind it isn't terribly serious about the page. And if the page owner isn't serious, why should the visitor take it seriously?

Further, if your posts are only getting one or two comments each (or worse yet, zero), it'll look kind of pathetic. It'll be dispiriting to the fans, and frankly, to you as the page owner as well. It's hard to get excited about doing two or three posts a week when you feel like the proverbial tree falling in the empty forest.

There's a huge difference between a few dozen fans and a

few hundred. A few thousand? Even better. The more fans you have, the greater your odds of getting a critical mass for community, and the greater the likelihood that a visitor will decide it's worth hanging out and becoming a fan themselves.

Here are some free (or cheap) steps you can take to drive up your fan base when getting started:

- **Ask your friends—especially Facebook friends—to become fans. Don't just ask politely, tell them you need them to do it so you can reach critical mass. Keep asking until you get at least a hundred.**

- **Promote it on other properties you have. Got a website? Put a prominent link on it. Got an email list? Ask them to become fans.**

- **Have a contest, where someone needs to be a fan to win. Even a small prize, such as a T-shirt, can provoke a click. You need to be careful with this one, since Facebook rules prohibit directly offering people compensation to become fans. However, you can require someone to be a fan in order to have a *chance* at winning a random drawing (make sure to check Facebook rules before you do this, however, since they can change).**

If you want to drive up your fan numbers quickly, consider placing some ads on Facebook. We'll get more into the specific details of Facebook ads in Chapter 18. But for now, here are some reasons why this may make sense for you, even if your budget is quite small:

- **You don't need a fortune to get started. Want to spend a few hundred dollars? Even less? It's possible with Facebook ads. Unlike many other ad options, you don't need a designer to create a great ad. If you've got a decent eye, can pick a good stock or clip art image, and you write a few sentences, you can create a very good ad. Further, there is no minimum purchase required. You decide your budget, and you pay either each time the ad is clicked, or each time it's viewed.**

- **A little goes a long way.** Facebook allows you to get unbelievably precise with your targeting, and given its massive size, even hyper-precise ads can still yield a good critical mass of targets. Want to reach self-identified country music fans in New York City? Facebook has nearly twenty thousand of them. Wine lovers in Des Moines? Facebook has over two thousand. Men interested in men in Fargo? There's over four hundred. If your targeting is done well, even a hundred dollars could yield you from dozens to hundreds of new fans.

If this sounds of interest, make sure to read Chapter 18 for specific tips on how craft, plan, and optimize your ads.

ADVANCED PAGE BUILDING

What I've described thus far are the basic steps to getting a good, solid Facebook page up and running. And for 90 percent of you, that will probably do the trick. But what if you want to get more elaborate? Perhaps you've seen some pages with custom landing places, as opposed to the wall, the tab with all the posts, where people land by default. Should you go that route?

Frankly, I'm skeptical of pages that get too elaborate and that draw people away from the wall. I understand the desire for a pretty page, and some of these pages really have some top-notch design. In some cases, getting a bit more elaborate might make sense. For example, the Lady Gaga page (Facebook.com/Lady Gaga) features music and videos—something that makes sense, and something she has the luxury of doing, given her already enormous, passionate fan base.

In general, however, I think it's a mistake for most pages to get too elaborate with design. Facebook works well in large part because the structure is clean and consistent, and users know what to expect when they come to a page. This is one of the reasons that Facebook has ultimately done so much better than MySpace, a site that allows for more user creativity and page manipulation, but which consequently leads to more confusion for new visitors. I'd strongly encourage you to avoid messing with a format that works.

Moreover, the wall is by far the most viral part of the page. That's where posts are shared, liked, and commented on, and those are the activities that spur viral spreading. It doesn't make a whole lot of sense to force people to land somewhere else before they can go there. Add other elements (tabs) if you want, but I'd strongly recommend keeping the wall as the default landing tab.

As long as you keep these things in mind, however, and as long as you keep your eye on the stats that matter (fans and inter- actions), there's nothing wrong with adding some more elements to your page, or experimenting a bit.

Probably the easiest way to expand the complexity of your page is to use the "Facebook Apps" option. These are plugins or applications, some created by Facebook and some by others, that can be added to fan pages. You can get to the apps section by clicking "Edit" when you are logged in and on your page, and then clicking on "Apps." This will bring up the apps that Face- book installs on each page by default (such as photos and videos and discussion boards), but will also give you the option to browse more at the bottom of the page.

The most flexible of these apps is the FBML one. Once you've installed it on your page, it creates an additional tab, and acts as a blank slate into which you can paste HTML code. Essentially, you can craft a basic web page within the tab. This is how most of the pages with custom landing spots create them. Once you've created the tab and put in the HTML code, that tab will show up with the other tabs in the left column. You can make that tab the default landing spot by changing the "default landing tab" when you are editing the page (though again, even though that's *how* you can do it, you really should consider *whether* it makes sense to do it). One note of caution, however: Facebook is transitioning away from the FBML app in favor of an iFrame approach. The basics are pretty much the same, allowing you to build a simple web page within a tab. But just be aware that you may need to search for an iFrame app instead of the FBML one when you are setting up your advanced page.

Beyond the FBML app, there are thousands upon thousands of others in the directory that can do all kinds of things. They do change on a regular basis, so I'd urge you to explore them on your own. One note of caution: Many of these apps can be installed by a page admin and begin working immediately. Others, however, also require a page visitor to install an app themselves before they can experience the enhanced functionality. People hate this. Don't do it. Don't force them to leap over hurdles.

FACEBOOK: TAKING PEER PRESSURE TO AN "11"

Peer pressure works. And right now, it's hard to find a better tool than Facebook for delivering peer pressure in a concentrated, focused, effective form.

Check out a popular fan page on Facebook, and you'll notice that it lists friends of yours who like it. When I view the "Starbucks" page, for example, it shows that fifty-five friends of mine like it. It even shows their faces at the top, in the list of fans.

Right off the bat, when I see that, I can't help but get drawn in. It's one thing if Starbucks is telling me something nice about itself. But it's a heck of a lot more compelling if my friends are endorsing that view. Remember the Yankelovich study cited in the introduction, about how 76 percent of consumers don't believe companies tell the truth in advertisements? Getting a thumbs-up from peers is much more convincing.

You might already have strong feelings about Starbucks, given the near ubiquity of the brand. But what about lesser-known or new products?

For those things, the impact is even more powerful. Suppose you weren't looking at the Starbucks page, but rather at the "Bob's Super Duper Coffee" page. You might normally just pass it by, ignoring it as just another piece of noise in the cacophony that is our lives. However, if you saw that twenty, thirty, fifty, or a hundred of your friends liked it, you'd probably stop for a moment and pay attention, right? At the very least, it might make you curious as to what it was that had attracted them. At most, it might make you favorably predisposed toward the brand yourself.

What if it were a restaurant in your neighborhood? One that you'd never tried before. If you saw the ad, it might attract and interest you, but you'd also know that it was an ad, and that the restaurant had paid for it. And thus, you'd be likely to take any nice things said in it with a grain of salt.

But if twenty, thirty, fifty, or a hundred of your friends liked it, that would send a powerful message. At a minimum, you'd think, "Hey, I probably could go there and not get food poisoning. Cool!" Beyond that, the more friends that liked it, the more likely you'd be to deem it an especially good place. Better food, cooler atmosphere, whatever. Bottom line, people whose opinions you trusted gave it the thumbs-up. And that would give the unknown brand trust by association, making the ad far, far more powerful.

We'll discuss ways to leverage Facebook's peer pressure even more in Chapters 18 and 19.

FACEBOOK POPS UP A LOT in this book, and with good reason. For nearly all the strategies I'll discuss, there simply is no better platform for getting your message read and spread than Facebook. It has made sharing unbelievably easy and friction free, and the targeting it enables is unprecedented and unmatched.

Facebook didn't exist a few years ago, and so it's certainly possible that some other competing system will displace it a few years from now. But right now, at this point in time, when it comes to spreading a message—Facebook really is the eight-hundred-terabyte gorilla.

shareretweetrepeatshareretweet
repeatshareretweetrepeatshare
etweetrepeatshareretweetrepeat

SIX

Using Twitter

Twitter is essentially a very stripped-down version of Facebook. Basically, it's just the status update. You can tell the world what you're doing, 140 characters at a time.

People decide which status updates they want to see by "following" someone who is of interest to them. It's akin to the Facebook fan page, in that following is one-directional. You will see updates (or "tweets") from the people you're following, but they won't see yours unless they follow you back.

Twitter is a great tool for one-to-many communications, and one that can be profoundly viral if the content tweeted is compelling. It allows you to hit your followers with information relatively instantly, and if they're logged on when you send that information, they'll see it right away. Unlike Facebook, there is no mysterious algorithm that controls what shows up in a feed. If someone is following you and you update your status, it will show up on their page, as will the updates from everyone they are following, ordered from most recent to oldest.

If people really, really like what you've said, they can easily "retweet" your message by clicking just below it. This will post what you sent them to all of *their* followers. One-click "cc all." If it's particularly compelling (for example, a phenomenal joke or perceptive observation), it might keep getting retweeted over and over again, by hundreds or even thousands of people.

Other tweeters can also mention you in a post or a response, something that will get your name (or more accurately, your Twitter handle) in front of their followers. For example, my Twitter handle is @JHlinko and my page can be viewed at Twitter .com/JHlinko. Let's say I post a tweet that catches the interest of @John_Doe. Here's how the exchange might go (notes in parentheses):

> **JHLINKO:** I just flew in from Reno and, boy, are my arms tired!

> **JOHN_DOE:** I can't believe @JHlinko used that lame joke! (Followers of John_Doe would see this tweet, and the @JHlinko would be hyperlinked back to my page, Twitter.com/JHlinko.)

> **JHLINKO:** Hey, you're the one that retweeted it! @John_Doe I can't believe @JHlinko used that lame joke! (My followers would now be able to click @John_Doe to go to his page.)

At this point, our followers might jump in and respond as well, if they felt so inclined. And those seeing my handle or John Doe's handle who don't already follow us might be compelled to do so now that we're on their radar.

That's the good part. And if you are a person or an organization that has compelling stuff to say, and if there already are lots of people who want to hear it, an aggressive Twitter strategy might be for you.

TOUGHER FOR BUILDING COMMUNITY

Where Twitter falls down a bit is in the difficulty in building community around content. A user can reply to another's tweet, but it can be tough to follow the trail. With Facebook, when you comment on a post, the comment is attached to that post. Whether you comment on it an hour later, a day later, or a year later, the context is clear. Further, a back-and-forth series of comments on that post from any number of users will have a clear context and flow. Finally, you get a notification when someone responds. Thus, it's very common for a compelling post to generate a conversation that gets dozens or even hundreds of posts in a few hours.

With Twitter, it's a little trickier. A response to a tweet will show up in the feed of the original tweeter. And if that original tweeter responds in kind, it will show up in the feed of the retweeter.

The real challenge, however, comes when someone else tries to insert themselves in the conversation. Taking the earlier example, with the "arms are tired" tweet, many people may respond to the original tweet, but it's a lot tougher for them to respond to each other in order, and get a real conversation going. It's doable, it just takes some more jumping around from page to page on the part of the tweeter. Facebook, with comments attached to a post, as in a blog, is much more intuitive for most users.

Bottom line, it's much tougher to get a long, sequential conversation happening on Twitter, and thus, it's pretty rare.

Hash Tags

Where community does often come together on Twitter, however, is in the use of hash tags, which begin with the symbol #. Initially, it was used as a way for people to easily find others who were discussing the same event. For example:

- I can't wait for the big game! #Superbowl

- Go Patriots! #Superbowl

- Wait, did she just flub the national anthem? #Superbowl

With this hash tag and the term "Superbowl," it becomes very easy for anyone to search for "#Superbowl" and immediately see the latest tweets. The hash tag is also hyperlinked in each tweet, so people can simply click on it to see what others are saying on the topic. This is a particularly helpful way for those bonding around a smaller event to create some community. Conferences, for example, often have their own hash tags, so attendees can comment on the event as they're experiencing it.

These days, however, hash tags are more often used as catalysts for creativity. Someone will introduce a tag, specifically to generate responses. For example, let's say I throw out the hash tag "#BadDesserts," as in "Bee lime pie #BadDesserts." Others would be prompted to respond with joke desserts of their own, such as "Vanilla Lice Cream #BadDesserts" or "Peanut Butt Cookies #BadDesserts." Some of these tags can really explode rapidly, getting to the point where they generate multiple tweets per second.

Fun, to be sure, but it's tough to leverage that flash community to your advantage. With Facebook, if you initiate a post that generates a lot of comments, all those comments are tied to your post, and you get the credit and traffic. With Twitter, you may initiate a hash tag that generates a million responses, but it's tough for people to know it was you unless others chose to mention you, or they dig to the bottom of the search.

Twitter also falls short of Facebook in a few key respects:

- **Sharing multimedia is not as seamless. You can attach pictures and videos, but unlike Facebook, where the item is right below the post, Twitter followers have to click to see what you shared.**

- **Twitter doesn't collect nearly as much demographic information as Facebook, meaning the same type of hyper targeting isn't possible.**

- It has only begun to allow some advertising, based on keywords. But Twitter seems to be rolling it out slowly, and it's pretty confusing to figure out *how to actually buy an ad*. Thus, paying to drive eyeballs and bump up your numbers is still not an option.

This doesn't mean Twitter is a waste of time. It's still a highly viral environment. And in fairness to Twitter, the company is constantly rolling out upgrades that address some of the shortfalls. It just means it has to be the right fit. Nearly anyone trying to get a message spread could likely make use of Facebook. Twitter can be fun for anyone, but is useful from a marketing standpoint to a much more selective audience.

TO TWEET OR NOT TO TWEET?

Here's a little test. Which describes you best?

1. You don't have an existing audience, nor one that will come to you on its own. You may very well have interesting things to say, but you'll need to find people who want to listen. You'll need to dig and search for an audience.

2. You have an existing audience, or an eminently natural potential one, that *already wants to hear* what you have to say. You're a celebrity or a well-known company, product, politician, author, etc. But if you tweet it, they will come.

If you fall into the first category, you might want to start off by simply feeding your Facebook updates in to Twitter. It's a fairly easy process. When logged in on Facebook, try going to Facebook.com/twitter (if that doesn't work, type "Twitter" into the Facebook Help search bar). At that point, you'll be invited to link any page you are an admin for to whatever Twitter account you choose. From then on, when you post a status update on that Facebook page, it will automatically show up on the Twitter page as well. It's a nice way to get something for nothing. Once you set it up—a five-minute process—you'll automatically be populating your Twitter feed at the same time. Even if just a few dozen people choose to follow it, that's fine, since you're not having to do anything to service them. And if the Twitter following does start growing, and you reach a critical mass of followers that makes it worth spending more time on this front to customize content for Twitter, that's a nice problem to have!

If you fall into category two, you may want to start off with a more aggressive strategy on Twitter. Key steps will include (1) creating optimized content for Twitter and (2) building a following so it actually gets seen.

CREATING OPTIMIZED CONTENT FOR TWITTER

If you choose to go beyond just feeding your Facebook page updates, and instead come up with content for Twitter specifically, there are a number of things to keep in mind.

Post at a Good Pace

With Twitter, you can actually post content even more often than with Facebook. A few times a day is fine. Some tweeters even go as far as a few times an hour, but at that point, you'd better have something really interesting to say, since you could end up showing up several times on the page when followers log on. There's nothing more likely to precipitate an "unfollow" than multiple posts that are all dull.

Get to the Point Quickly

With Twitter, you've got just 140, so you need to get to your point even more quickly. But don't even use the entire 140 characters. Keep it to 120 or less. If people retweet your post, they may want to add something up front (even if it's just the customary "RT"). Let them.

Make It Interesting and Provocative

Remember, you want your post to be spread-worthy. Whatever you do, don't put up a post that's a yawner, just because you feel the need to post something.

Make the Content Appropriate for Social Media

As with Facebook, this is not just a medium for making announcements or posting press releases, it's one for spurring conversation. Don't come across as stiff and overly PR-ish or, frankly, full of BS. Fans aren't following you for ads packaged as posts. Ask them questions. Get their feedback. And don't just talk about yourself; throw out topics from the news for conversation.

Engage with Your Followers

Don't just post and run, make sure to reply and retweet yourself. If someone replies to you, reply back. Do a search a few times a day, and if you see someone mention you as part of their post, or mention the topic you're focused on, reply to them as well.

Ask Fans Directly to Retweet the Post

There's nothing wrong with being blatant, especially if you can work in a logical reason for sharing:

- **My new wine store is open! Free wine tasting this Tuesday! RT and spread the word!**

- **Earth Day is this weekend! Stop by and learn how you can save the Earth. We will plant a tree for each retweet of this!**

- **Follow @LeftAction. Every time this is retweeted, an angel gets its wings, and a Republican loses its horns.**

Think in Terms of "Short Update and Link to More"

You don't have a lot of characters to work with, but if you've got a website (or even a Facebook page), there's no reason you can't hook people on Twitter, and drive them to those properties with more extensive text. Think of it in terms of one of those "next up" teasers that always precedes nightly newscasts or late night shows. Give them something that compels them to click over. Use one of the URL-shortening services, such as TinyURL.com, to save precious space in your tweet when including a URL: "Bananas the size of Buicks? http://tinyurl.com/BananaWOW."

Include Links to Pictures, Video, and Audio

Although the presentation isn't as rich as in Facebook, where the multimedia is embedded in the actual post, the promise of a compelling picture or video can be enough to spark a click over.

See What's "Trending" and Ride the Wave

Twitter lists "trending" topics, basically, what's being tweeted about the most at that point in time. Typically, it's highly topical stuff, often that which is breaking in the news. Get in the habit of seeing what's trending and figuring out if you can post relevant content that rides that wave. If you see one of the creative hash tags trending, try to leverage it.

For example, let's say "#SexiestActor" was trending. You could post something like "We think Robert DeNiro is the #SexiestActor, but what is the sexiest wine? http://tinyurl.com/SexiestWine" (link to your wine shop site). Now anyone searching for #SexiestActor would see your plug (for a few minutes, that is, until more content pushed it down the page).

BUILDING A TWITTER FOLLOWING

Until Twitter advertising is more established, building a big following through paying to drive people toward your feed really isn't an option. Nevertheless, there are still steps you can take to help jump-start your following.

Promote the Heck Out of Your Feed

Link to it from your website. Email it to your list. Promote it from your Facebook page. Let people know it exists!

Start Following Other People

When you follow someone else's feed, they get an email informing them that "@JohnDoe is now following you on Twitter." Some percentage of those people will decide to start following you back.

Start Following Reporters

Find reporters who follow your industry, sector, or other focus, and start following them. Again, some percentage will start following you back. And hey, if you tweet something interesting and they see it, there's a chance they might mention you in a story or contact you for more information. I've had that happen and can say firsthand that there are few things more satisfying than having a quick 140-character tweet blossom into a sweet media story.

Search for Keywords, and Follow People Whose Tweets Contain Those Words

Let's say you're a writer trying to promote your poetry. A quick search of people mentioning "poetry" in their profile yields a huge number of accounts, ranging from "Poetry News" to "The New Yorker" to legions of individuals who simply have an affinity for poetry. Go ahead and follow them, since, again, some percentage will follow you back.

Want to go beyond the basics and get creative? Start engaging followers in quirkier, more creative ways—ways that really stand out. My favorite example? The Old Spice Guy.

OLD SPICE GUY

If you've been in the United States and you have a TV, the odds are good that you've seen the "Old Spice Guy" TV ad. Played brilliantly by actor Isaiah Mustafa, a handsome, well-built former football player, the Old Spice Guy hilariously runs through a series of quick set changes, all "dream man" clichés, and reminds his viewers that, "even if your man can't look like me, he can still smell like me with Old Spice."

The commercial gained wide acclaim, even winning a Primetime Emmy Award for Outstanding Commercial. It became a YouTube sensation, garnering over thirty million views in just a few months.

But what Old Spice did next really took it into the stratosphere and into the annals of "Twistory." The company began directly engaging fans via Twitter. Not only via tweets, but through a series of rapidly produced videos featuring the Old Spice Guy, done in response to the tweets of others. It sent tweets to big-name stars, but also average fans with smaller followings, with a link to a video aimed personally at them. Naturally, these folks were blown away to get a response from the Old Spice Guy himself and spread the video responses like wildfire.

The best one of all started with a request from a man on Twitter asking the Old Spice Guy to propose to the man's girlfriend on his behalf. Just a few hours later—lighting fast in video production terms—a tweet was posted on the Old Spice page, linking viewers to a video of the Old Spice Guy himself, making the proposal. And it wasn't just a plain old proposal. It was a hilariously over-the-top proposal, complete with candles, a ring, and mood lighting.

Oh, and a short while later, via a tweet, the world got the good news: She said yes.

The results? Rather mind-blowing. In one week, Twitter followers of Old Spice increased tenfold, from fewer than four thousand followers to nearly forty thousand. Mentions of "Old Spice" on Twitter jumped into the thousands per day, including one absolutely astonishing day (the proposal) with over sixty thousand.

All of this was on behalf of a brand that had previously been best known as "the stuff your grandpa smells like."

Pretty incredible. And over a year later, "Old Spice" is still generating multiple mentions per hour on Twitter, and the marketing campaign specifically is still mentioned multiple times per day. It was quite simply a brilliant and brilliantly effective use of Twitter.

Granted, Old Spice didn't do this for free. It worked because they'd built brand recognition for the Old Spice Guy through a fair amount of TV advertising. Nevertheless, the amount they spent for the Twitter portion of the campaign was relatively small. They easily could've shown the TV ads, basked in the great reaction, and been done with it. But they went a step further, got creative, and spurred a viral firestorm.

GEORGETOWN CUPCAKE

Even if you're not a billion-dollar brand, you can still enhance your Twitter effectiveness by getting a bit creative—and by giving followers something useful.

It's become quite common, for example, for sidewalk street vendors to tweet their day's location to followers. For a dime-a-dozen hot dog vendor, this might not be compelling. But some of the more creative vendors (with especially yummy offerings) have developed passionate followings.

My favorite Twitter use by a "little guy," however, has to be Georgetown Cupcake (Twitter.com/GtownCupcake). It started off as a small shop in Washington, DC, that sold very tasty cupcakes, often with a creative spin (with flavors such as "pumpkin spice" and "salted caramel"). Still though, even with the creativity, it was basically just another neighborhood bakery.

What the store did (and still does) with Twitter, however, was rather brilliant. Each morning, it started sending out a tweet with a "secret flavor" cupcake, that is, a flavor not on the menu. The first one hundred customers who came in and asked for the secret flavor got one of those cupcakes for free. People loved it and started following their Twitter account like crazy. And every morning, just after the tweet was sent out, there would be a line out the door of people waiting to claim their cupcake. The store's Twitter following quickly shot up from the hundreds to the thousands.

Yes, there was a cost for this to the store. Cupcakes don't come free. However, it was lower than it might seem at first glance, given that a sizable chunk of the visitors picked up more than one cupcake during their visit, and an even more sizable chunk popped by at other times, when buying a dozen cupcakes for a birthday party, office party, or just for the heck of it. And of course, people told their friends about it, leading to new customers. It was fun. It was spread-worthy.

But the benefit didn't stop there. A line out the door each morning sent quite a market signal to people passing by. It said loud and clear that there was something special about this place, and that the cupcakes must really be awesome (especially given that there were several other shops within walking distance that also sold cupcakes and had no lines). Not surprisingly, some portion of those passersby joined the line themselves. In short order, there was a line out the door from the shop nearly every day, regardless of time.

And the benefit didn't stop there either! The buzz generated even more buzz, and soon the shop was picked as the setting for a reality show on TLC (a cable network) called *DC Cupcakes*. That's right. A reality show—about cupcakes. Incredible.

The store now has multiple locations, lines are still out the door, and its Twitter followers are now measured in the *tens of thousands*.

YES, TWITTER HAS SOME LIMITATIONS, especially when compared to Facebook. But that's a pretty high bar for judgment, and there's a reason why Twitter is still a big, big deal. If you have something very compelling to say, and you have a particularly creative way of saying it, one of the places you should be saying it is definitely Twitter.

SEVEN

Setting Up a Blog

Many people wonder whether it makes sense to launch a blog as part of their marketing efforts, either as a supplement to their website or as their main website.

For those not familiar with blogs, a blog is basically a website structured as a diary (the name actually comes from the shortened version of "web log"). Typically, posts are displayed on the home page in the order that the blogger posts them, from newest to oldest. Visitors to the site can leave comments on the post. This is generally supplemented by additional, static content in sidebars, a la a normal website.

Whether it makes sense for you to start a blog really depends on three things:

1. **What you expect to get from the blog**

2. **Whether you're just using it as an easy platform for a website, or an actual blog**

3. **If you're using it as an actual blog, your willingness and ability to keep it updated**

Because there are a few high-profile blogs that get enormous amounts of traffic, some people erroneously assume that a blog can be used to quickly generate traffic for them. But again, a blog is just a website by another name. It is certainly better for building community, given that it allows for comments in context. But if you are expecting a magic wave of traffic from out of the blue, think again. There are already a few hundred million blogs out there, and no one is waking up in the morning looking for a new one.

If you are simply looking for an easier way to build your website, then using a blog platform could certainly make sense. WordPress, TypePad, Blogger, and other systems offer a relatively easy way for even a novice to get a quality site up quickly, as we saw in Chapter 3.

If, on the other hand, you really intend to use it as a blog, with regularly updated content, then you should expect to do a fair amount of work before you start yielding the rewards of strong traffic and engaged visitors and commenters. Most important, you should be willing to put up a new post at least once a week, and ideally a few times a week. These posts will need to be more substantive than Facebook or Twitter posts. A pithy line or two won't do, if you wish to get visitors coming back often. A few hundred words is more typical.

A good test to determine if a blog is for you is to try to come up with a dozen posts before you launch the blog. You don't need to actually write out the full posts, just try to come up with headlines and a few sentences describing what the post would be about. If you're an artist, this could be samples of your art. If you're a writer or journalist, then your writing would be the logical choice. Running a wine shop? Reviews of different wines would certainly make sense.

If you are able to come up with a dozen posts without a whole lot of work and effort, that's a good sign that you've got enough to say to warrant a blog. It's also a sign that you might want to consider using a blog as your main site, since a constantly refreshed site is frankly more engaging and interesting than a static one.

If, on the other hand, you can't think of a dozen posts, you may want to think twice about doing a blog. A dozen posts at one post a week is less than three months' worth of posts. If you genuinely find yourself struggling to get that many ideas, the odds are that you'll start to really run dry after a month or two and will find coming up with new content to be a real burden. Given that your blog will still be new, and not yet have an audience, you might find yourself really struggling with very little reward.

Be honest with yourself. If you can't come up with good, updated ideas on a regular basis, you may get more bang for the buck by focusing your effort elsewhere, such as Facebook (where updates can be much shorter, and where it's much easier to build a critical mass of commenters).

OPTIMIZING YOUR BLOG

If you decide to plunge ahead with your blog, there are a few things you should do to optimize your effort.

Take Time to Craft Quality Content

If you can come up with high-quality pieces of your own—stories, reviews, work samples—that's great. Alternatively, your blog could be more a reporting one, taking snippets of breaking or interesting content (with links to the full story) with your commentary attached.

Include Easy Ways for People to Share the Content

This should include icons for sharing on Facebook, Twitter, and whatever else comes along. Again, AddThis is a good, easily installable tool for doing this.

Make Sure Your Titles and URLs for the Blog Posts Are Optimized for Searching

Specifically, separate the words in the articles, so they can be picked up by search engines. For example, "SampleMonkeyBlog .com/great-banana-recipes" versus "SampleMonkeyBlog.com/ greatbananarecipes."

Keep the Content Reasonably Fresh

Even if you can't do it regularly, try not to let the posts get more than a week out of date. If you have "evergreen" content (stuff that really isn't tied to current news stories or dates), you can even use the trick of "recycling" once in a while, changing the dates on old posts to resurface them at the top.

See What People Respond to, and Do More of It

Keep an eye on statistics and see which posts are getting the most views, as well as links from other sites. Also, keep an eye on which ones are generating the most comments. See what works, and keep doing more of it.

INTEGRATING YOUR BLOG WITH YOUR SOCIAL MEDIA EFFORT

Once you have your blog up and running, you'll want to drive traffic toward it, to build a critical mass. For the most part, you can do this for your blog through the same tactics you'd use for any website—paid advertising, PR, links from your site, announcements to your email list, and all the other tactics used for getting folks to aim their eyeballs somewhere for at least a fleeting moment.

Beyond the usual steps, however, blogs are especially well suited to marketing (and cross-marketing) via Facebook and Twitter. Both blogs and those platforms are fueled by frequent updates. On Twitter and Facebook, however, optimal updates are fairly short ones. Sometimes, you will want to say more. This is where your blog can come in handy.

Let's say you're a wine store owner, and you're writing a blog about wine, "Grapest Story Ever Told." You've decided to write a four-hundred-word post about the best Cabernets under $10 a bottle. A perfect length for a blog post, but too long for a Twitter or Facebook update. No problem. Once you've got your post up, just use the "short update and link to more" approach talked about earlier: "Best Cabernets under $10? Learn which ones: http://GrapestStoryEverTold.com/cheap-cabs."

It's simple and straightforward, but it lets those on your Twitter and Facebook feeds know you've got a new post, and puts them one click away from reading it if they find the teaser intriguing. If you do this on a regular basis, as a matter of habit, the marketing push can work both ways, as your readers now will have a good reason to sign up for your Twitter or Facebook updates. They may not want to go out of their way to visit your blog on a regular basis, but may be more than happy to have the teaser show in their feed, so they can make the decision whether they want to visit on a case-by-case basis.

Not surprisingly, a lot of news organizations are now taking this route with Twitter. For example, here's a sampling of tweets from CNN (Twitter.com/CNN):

- **Marilyn Monroe photos found at garage sale still a mystery.** http://on.cnn.com/kUqQs7

- **USDA to replace food pyramid with plate icon, source says.** http://on.cnn.com/jFLsTY

- **10 fascinating Facebook facts—and what they say about us.** http://on.cnn.com/j2xHgQ

The odds are at least one of these would be intriguing enough to provoke a click. Given that CNN has several million followers on Twitter, that's a heck of a lot of clicks.

You may not be able to get millions of followers clicking over to your blog post, but if you can get hundreds or even dozens for this minimal effort, it's well worth it.

"CALLING DR. KEVORKIAN"

Finally, if you get to a point where your blog is sucking an enormous amount of time and energy, and you're not seeing enough traffic and visitors to make it worth the effort, you may want to consider stepping back, and either shutting down the blog or putting it in "100 percent recycle" mode. That is, just move exclusively into the mode of changing dates on old posts to resurface them. If you're running a breaking-news blog, this obviously won't work. But if you're doing poetry, art, reviews, or something else where the content is not time sensitive, repeating posts should be fine. Granted, you probably won't build up regular readers, since "repeats" are never as interesting the second time around. But if you've tried already, and it's not working, better to focus your efforts elsewhere than to get caught up in the blog vortex.

A BLOG CAN BE A great way to express yourself and a great way to promote your brand. But if you choose to blog, go in with your eyes open and recognize that it will take a significant amount of work before you are likely to start yielding benefits.

Take the plunge if you dare, but make sure you don't end up in a situation where you're putting in a lot of effort for little reward. You should own your blog—your blog shouldn't own you.

PART THREE

CRAFTING VIRAL MESSAGES

The technology may have changed, and the optimal paths for delivering content may have evolved, but when it comes down to it, *content is still king*. Content is ultimately the "virus."

We've already touched upon crafting your message earlier in this book, in terms of tactical dos and don'ts for specific platforms. But let's move out of the realm of platform-specific tactics, and explore what makes a message spread-worthy in general. What would make it more likely to go viral, regardless of platform?

This section will examine general techniques, dive into specifics on some especially useful fronts, and finally describe how you can test your messages for virality.

EIGHT

Making Your Messages
Spread-Worthy

Want your content to go viral? That's easy. Just make it awesome. Got that? Great, end of chapter.

Okay, so I'm being a bit flip here, but it's important to keep this in mind, because it's true. It's all too easy to get wrapped up in the technology and the techniques and forget the big picture. The content that consistently spreads the most and the quickest is the content that is the most awesome. That is, the funniest, the most emotionally impactful, the most shocking, the most interesting, or simply awesome in some other "know it when you see it" way.

I never cease to be amazed by how much truly mediocre content is put out via the Internet. Many of the same people who would agonize for weeks over a speech to fifty people think nothing of rushing through an email to five thousand. And this holds true not just for individuals, but for large, well-resourced entities as well. Read the last few emails you received from big companies, organizations, or political figures. Were they awesome? Did you feel the urge to spread them? Probably not. What a wasted opportunity!

Don't fall into this trap. Take the time to really craft content that is compelling, interesting, and as close to awesome as you can make it. Use the tips in this chapter, get help from friends who are creative and good storytellers, and take the time to do it right.

THE 118TH EMAIL TEST

You've crafted an email to send to your list. Before you hit the button, imagine the following scenario. Picture one of your intended targets. Imagine that target has just come back from a hard day at work, has 117 emails in the inbox, and yours was number 118—buried somewhere in the middle. Would it get read? Would it grab the recipient right away? Is it novel? Compelling?

Is it awesome?

Be honest with yourself and run it by some friends and colleagues you know would be honest with you as well. If your message feels like something that would get lost in the din of 118 emails, then the odds are that it would probably get lost among 18 or 8 emails as well.

If it doesn't pass the test, go back and redo it. And of course, this goes for Facebook posts and tweets as well—if someone has 118 items in their feed, does yours get read?

It's a high bar, for sure, but given the potential rewards for going viral, "awesome" is a bar worth jumping for.

MAKE YOUR MESSAGE NOVEL

If you want your message to spread, include something new and novel as part of it. People like to spread news, and you can't spell "news" without "new."

In his book *Purple Cow*, Seth Godin explains this wonderfully through the example of, well, a purple cow. If you were driving out from the city into the country, you'd notice the first cow you saw. "Wow! A cow! I'm in the country! Yee haw!" You'd probably notice the second cow. Maybe the third. But the hundred and third? Probably not. Unless of course it were purple. That, you'd notice. And in the same vein, if you give your followers information that's truly new and novel, they'll notice it, and they'll be a heck of a lot more likely to spread it.

This holds true beyond the web as well. Think of the example of Larry Doby. Baseball fans may know him as a fine player whose career spanned the 1940s and 1950s. You may not have heard of him, but you've almost certainly heard of one of his contemporaries—Jackie Robinson. The big difference? Jackie Robinson broke the color barrier in Major League Baseball, becoming the first African-American player of the modern era. Larry Doby was the second, starting eleven weeks after Robinson. Ever heard of Bert Hinkler? He was the second person to fly solo across the Atlantic Ocean. Odds are better that you've heard of the guy who preceded him, Charles Lindbergh.

But you don't have to make history to be novel. In my own experience, one of the most explosively viral Facebook pages I've created is called "Not Having George Bush as President." It's got over half a million fans and climbing, all without a marketing budget. What made it spread? The fact that it had the word "not" at the beginning. At a time when fan pages were new, there were pages for all kinds of things, including countless ones targeted at Democratic activists. But being a fan of "not something" was new, quirky, and eye-catching. People in the target audience found it amusing, and thought it was spread-worthy enough to tell friends about.

A few months later, a simple search of Facebook pages starting with "Not Having" yielded dozens of results, particularly on the activism front. However, while many did quite well, none came anywhere close to the success of the first page. The silly twist of a phrase, initially devastatingly effective, was simply no longer novel.

Another one of the most viral efforts I've been involved with was ActForLove.org, an online dating site launched in 2003. It was far from the first online dating site to market—more like the thousand and first. But it had a novel spin—it was a dating site specifically for activists. The slogan? "Take action, get action."

That simple twist turned it from just another dating site to something new, novel, and thus worthy of attention. With almost no marketing budget, it quickly grew to tens of thousands of members, and was featured in the *New York Times*, the *Washington Post*, *Newsweek*, and a slew of other publications.

Yoram Bauman is one of my favorite stand-up comics. I've never actually heard him do a routine, but the mere fact that he describes himself as "the world's first and only stand-up economist" strikes me as brilliant. And memorable, even years after I first saw his site.

Whatever you're doing, and whatever you're publicizing, think hard whether you can come up with a novel spin.

RIDE AN EXISTING WAVE

If you've ever surfed, known a surfer, or even just seen that classic *Brady Bunch* episode where the gang goes to Hawaii, you know that surfing requires a wave. Sure, it's possible to create one by splashing your own hands, but it's a heck of a lot more efficient to ride the one that the ocean has already produced. If you're looking for virality, keep this in mind when you craft your content. *Try to ride an existing wave.*

Hot News

Is there something big in the news? Some national or world event? Something relevant to your topic specifically? Try to make your message relevant to that story. We've seen in Chapter 6 the example of riding Twitter trending topics, but this is something you can do with real-life "trending topics" as well.

Back in 2006, a colleague of mine, Mike Panetta, was trying

to think of a way to promote voting rights for the people of Washington, DC (who do not have the right to vote for members of Congress). Noticing that the winter Olympics were about to begin, Mike came up with the brilliant idea of trying to field a winter Olympic team for DC. If the people of DC didn't have full voting rights, he reasoned, they really weren't part of America, and if they really weren't part of America . . . they deserved their own, separate Olympic team!

He chose curling, a sport in which the athletes hurl stones down an ice path, and teammates frantically sweep the ice with brooms to slow down and speed up the stone (honestly, it sounds insane, but it's quite fun). A group of us donned uniforms, got out on the ice, curled, and got a heck of a lot of attention—all while preaching about DC voting rights the whole time.

It was a brilliant twist that generated enormous news coverage—riding shotgun on the ubiquitous Olympics stories of those few weeks—and hundreds of thousands of page views for an accompanying website. But without riding the Olympic wave, it would've simply been dismissed as yet another tired campaign for voting rights and, frankly, been largely ignored.

Calendar Events

Keep an eye out for holidays, sporting events, and other special days you can peg your content to. And go beyond the major holidays (Christmas, Hanukkah, July Fourth, etc.) and try to ride on some playful ones.

Promoting a bakery? Why not offer a two-for-one pie special on March 14 ($3/14$ = 3.14 = pi)? Sure, it's a groaner, but it'll get noticed, and getting noticed is half the battle.

Cultural References and Icons

Can you play off a popular TV show or commercial? A known icon? A scandal? All of these things can become the "host mechanism" upon which your content can ride. No matter how big your marketing effort already is, it can be made even bigger and more effective by riding this kind of wave. Dennis Dennehy is one of the top marketing mavens in the world of music, having driven astonishingly successful publicity campaigns over twenty years for artists ranging from Lady Gaga to Eminem to Gwen Stefani. And even at this level, he is keenly attuned to the power of viral marketing. "Almost every piece of visual content we release by an artist we hope has some type of viral spread that engages both the fan base and the curious," Dennehy said.[10]

You may have seen Vince the ShamWow! Guy on the ubiquitous infomercials for that product. Well, according to YouTube, hundreds of thousands of you have also seen the hysterical parody ad that Vince did for a new Eminem album, where he used the CD to slice and dice cheese, onions, and even a silicon implant. Eminem may already be one of the top artists on the planet, but even he can benefit from riding a viral wave. Marketing geniuses such as Dennehy take that lesson to heart, and so should you.

Keep an eye out for stories on the news and entertainment fronts, see what's hot, and see if you can ride it with your message. I find the *Huffington Post* to be a good source for this, since it straddles news and entertainment, and since you can tell by the volume of comments on a story just how "hot" it really is.

Internet Memes

Every day, there's some new hot (and generally weird) meme spreading on the Internet. And every few weeks, there is one that really explodes. Parodies of these memes can really ride on their traction.

You might be familiar, for example, with the "Rickroll," the rather odd practical joke of getting someone to click on an ostensibly important link, only to be taken to a video by '80s pop star Rick Astley (a video with thirty-three million views and counting). But did you know that there are literally hundreds of parodies of that video, cumulatively with tens of millions of views?

Taking the bakery example again, how much fun would it be to offer a free roll to any customer who would actually sing the

Astley song? Silly, yes, but the kind of silly that people spread the word about.

Be on the lookout as well for ways to combine Internet memes and cultural references. In 2011, T-Mobile, a mobile communications company, decided to create a video in conjunction with the wedding of Prince William and Kate Middleton. It was a huge event that was already making headlines around the world, and its viral power as a cultural reference was huge. What T-Mobile did next, however, really took it to the next level. The company used doubles of the royal family, and had them act out an Internet sensation from a few years earlier—a video of an actual wedding party entering the church dancing wildly to a high-energy pop song. The combination proved wildly successful, with the video quickly generating tens of millions of views on YouTube.

USE A VILLAIN

There's nothing like a good conflict to engage people, and you need a villain to build conflict. It's why villains have been a part of storytelling since stories were first told.

Do you have a natural villain? Someone your target audience already doesn't like? Use them! One of the most iconic TV ads ever was Apple's "1984" ad (referenced in Chapter 1), in which the top dog in the computer industry at the time (IBM) was put in the role of Orwell's "Big Brother." People loved the David versus Goliath element, and the chatter was incredible.

In my own experience building Facebook.com/LeftAction, a Facebook page geared toward Democratic activists, it took a lot of hard work and time to build the page to one hundred thousand fans. Two other pages I started, however, "Telling Dick Cheney to Shut the Hell Up" and "Telling Rush Limbaugh He's Full of Crap" hit more than double that number with far less effort. They were reaching exactly the same target audience I was trying to reach with Left Action, but the addition of figures this audience perceived as villains made these pages far more viral.

BUILD AN ONGOING NARRATIVE

Ever watch a soap opera? Generally the writing and the acting leave a lot to be desired. And yet, because the stories have an ongoing narrative, they're naturally engaging. It's hard to tear yourself away. They draw you in, and they keep you drawn in day after day, to see what happens.

Make your content do the same. Don't just write one-off emails or posts and then move on to the next story. Build an ongoing narrative that spans across messages.

Consider Contests That Span Over a Few Days or Weeks

One of my political clients did an "Ass Clown of the Year" contest targeting particularly troublesome political opponents. It was done via a daily poll over the course of a week, in which the lowest finisher was dropped each day. Juvenile? You bet! But engaging and traffic inducing? And a tactic that got people in the habit of coming back to his blog on a daily basis? Oh yes! I now routinely do the same with caption contests and polls on Facebook.

Provide Reports on Progress to Build Excitement

Running an effort with numbers attached? Petition campaign? Sales for a new product? Provide regular updates that show momentum and growth. One of my favorite tactics with Facebook pages, for example, is to post a thank-you update when they hit certain fan number milestones (say, one thousand, five thousand, etc.). For example, "Wow, in just one week, we've already hit a thousand fans! Thank you so much! Please give yourself a 'like' for all you've done!" It's fun, it's nice, and it's exciting for fans to know they're a part of something with momentum.

Give a Shout-Out in a Subsequent Message for Engagement on the Current One

For example, if you had a Facebook page promoting your ACME Widget product, you can post something like: "Fill in the blank.

'Before I give up my ACME Widget, I'd give up_____.' We'll give a shout-out to the comment that gets the most likes." On Twitter, you can do the same thing, but with a shout-out promised to the person with the best response (include a hash tag to keep track). Small thing, but it encourages people to participate, as well as to come back and see who won.

THESE ARE ALL GOOD GENERAL tips for increasing the spread-worthiness of your content—and doing so without having to break the bank, or hardly even break a sweat. Refer back to them often as you craft your message and see if there are ways to incorporate them to make the message more spread-worthy.

NINE

Using Humor

Humor may be funny, but when it comes to your viral marketing strategy, it's a very serious tool in your arsenal. *There may be no type of content that is more spread-worthy than well-crafted humor.* And yet, too many people dismiss humor as a tactic, especially if they are trying to convey a serious point. They make the assumption that if that content is funny, it can't make a serious impact as a tactic.

This is a huge mistake.

WHY HUMOR MATTERS

There's a reason sitcoms and funny movies and stand-up comedy clubs exist—people like humor. Humor is memorable. Think of your top five favorite TV ads ever. At least one of them is funny, right? In fact, I wouldn't be surprised if all five were.

From a marketing standpoint, humor is also important because it acts as a powerful weapon against cynicism. Remember that Yankelovich survey discussed in the introduction? The one showing that 76 percent of consumers don't believe companies tell the truth in advertisements? Most consumers have an instinctive wall of cynicism they put up when a marketing message is coming their way. But it's hard to maintain that wall when you're laughing. Humor is disarming, and for at least a moment, it allows you to pierce that wall of cynicism and have a chance to get your message through.

Most important of all, people *spread* humor. *A lot.* Think of all the emails that have ever been forwarded to you. What percentage of them were humorous? A pretty sizable amount, I'm betting, right? People like spreading humor. It's fun, it breaks up the day, and it makes them look cool.

Remember the "Old Spice Guy" TV ad? Thirty million views and counting on YouTube. That is far from the exception. Search for "TV ads" on YouTube and see which ones are getting the most views. Invariably, humorous ads will make up a huge share. And it was peer-to-peer sharing that drove up these view counts.

Think about that. People who normally ignore ads, primarily because they think they're full of BS, are not only watching *these* ads, they're spreading them like crazy.

Not every issue or product lends itself to humor. But nearly all do. Take breast cancer, for example. A laugh a minute, right? Um, no. It's a deadly serious issue, quite literally, one with an enormous amount of emotion attached to it. And yet, even for that, there is a place for humor.

THE NATIONAL BREAST CANCER COALITION: "GOLDEN BOOB" AWARD

A few years back, I had the honor of working with the National Breast Cancer Coalition, an outstanding organization fighting this horrible disease. NBCC is a highly effective organization, winning legislative battles one by one and advancing the fight against breast cancer. But at the time, it was doing so without a lot of attention and exposure. It was a quietly effective organization, with little ego and need for the spotlight.

For this reason, NBCC found it particularly irksome when others shamelessly exploited the disease for their own profit or unrelated political agendas. NBCC wanted to make this point, and call these people out for what they were doing. The typical approach of an advocacy organization would be something along the lines of the following:

- **Write an email saying why people should be outraged.**

- **Send that email, with the word "outraged" spread throughout it.**

- **Annoy recipients, who though logically supportive, frankly have outrage fatigue.**

NBCC took a different approach. They created the "Golden Boob Award," an award to "honor" the entity most shamelessly exploiting breast cancer for its own ends. The award ("the boobie") was a simple digital image that appeared on a small site designed for it, GoldenBoob.org (no longer active). It was an homage to the Oscar award, only with cleavage. The nominees were chosen by NBCC and put up to a vote on the website.

The winner was a group claiming (without any evidence) that abortion leads to breast cancer. It was a particular incendiary issue, one on which people can surely have different opinions, of course, but the tie-in to breast cancer had no factual basis.

NBCC's approach was daring, but it was also very fresh, funny, and memorable. The results? Fantastic:

- **Thousands of mentions online, and a big burst of traffic for NBCC.**

- **NBCC members loved it. It was fun, it was funny, and it was an example of fighting back, and *fighting back hard*.**

- The "winner" was absolutely outraged, complaining and sending angry letters. But remember the point in Chapter 8 about using a villain? Well, let's just say angering this villain brought all kinds of joy to supporters of NBCC.

If humor can be used to promote the cause of fighting breast cancer, then it really can be used for almost anything, right? Remember that the next time some joy sponge (see Chapter 21) tries to torpedo your funny marketing idea because an effort is "too serious" for humor.

Even in cases where humor is not the prime driver, it can be very effective as an added "spice" for the main effort. Remember the ActForLove.org example in Chapter 8? The online dating site for activists? Yes, it got attention because it was a new spin. But time and time again, it was the cheeky slogan, "take action, get action" that people repeated when they spread it and that caught reporters' attention when I pitched it. The DC Olympic team, from Chapter 8? The Olympic angle made it relevant to the news cycle of that time, but the choice in particular of curling, a sport that seems laughably ludicrous to those who don't understand it ("Why the hell are those people sweeping the ice?") really made it spread-worthy.

WHAT MAKES SOMETHING FUNNY?

So how do you make something funny? For advice on this, I turned to two of the funniest people in the humor business: Fred Armisen, star of *Saturday Night Live*, and Kevin Bleyer, Emmy Award–winning writer for *The Daily Show with Jon Stewart*. These guys clearly know the art of funny. And yet, even they have a tough time honing in on precisely where funny comes from.

As Bleyer put it, "Philosophizing about comedy is like dancing about architecture. Anyone who says they know precisely what makes something funny is kidding themselves."

Armisen gave a similar answer when asked what makes

something funny: "I think that's different for every person. It's an obvious answer I know, but it varies so much and it's kind of great. It also changes every day."

So is all lost? Is there no method to the madness?

Hardly. Even if we can't come up with the secret formula to making your funny bone tingle every time, we can hone in on which types of humor are most spreadable.

MAKING HUMOR SPREAD-WORTHY

When it comes to getting noticed, getting a reaction, and getting spread, "revelatory" humor may be the most powerful of all. Humor which is not just funny, but makes people want to shout, "Oh yeah! That's so true!" or "Yes! That's exactly what I've been thinking!" As the *Daily Show*'s Bleyer notes, "My email seems to fill up if we've somehow managed to crystallize a thought that many people have had but haven't been able to express."

Bleyer cited the example of some of the *Daily Show*'s coverage of the 2008 Republican convention, and in particular a segment showing the discrepancy between conservative pundit's Bill O'Reilly's scathing commentary on teenage pregnancy among teenage celebrities (calling Jamie Lynn Spears a "pinhead," for example), while suggesting just a few weeks later that the media should leave pregnant Bristol Palin alone, since she's just a girl who made a mistake. The segment spliced the two dueling O'Reillys together to show in splendid form just how much he'd flip-flopped. Folks who suspected O'Reilly had a double standard suddenly had the aha moment of seeing it before their eyes. "We pointed out that hypocrisy, and the Internet approved," said Bleyer.

The Internet approved all right. That video is *still* the single most viewed video on the *Daily Show* website (TheDailyShow .com), with more than four million views (not to mention many more on YouTube).

In my own experience, one of the most viralized advocacy

efforts I've worked with was for a client who decided to take on members of Congress railing against "government health care" (in the context of a healthcare reform bill) by playfully reminding them that Congress itself had government-sponsored health care, and asking them to "repeal their own health care first." It was amusing, and right on message since it exposed a basic level of hypocrisy that wasn't as apparent at first glance. Again, it gave that "aha" moment to all those who'd been trying to verbalize why these members were hypocritical. And it spread like wildfire.

Of course, this type of humor also spread both because it rode the wave of current events, and because it took on villains—tactics pointed out already in Chapter 8. These tactics are even more effective when combined with humor.

Riding a wave is, of course, the whole modus operandi of the *Daily Show*—just-in-time lampooning of what is hot in the news at that very moment. And as SNL's Armisen points, out, while he performs as a range of characters in all kinds of skits, it's his imitations of President Obama and New York Governor Paterson that people have brought up to him most often on the street. And of course, who can forget Tina Fey's impression of Sarah Palin during the 2008 campaign? Years later, people are still parroting Fey's phrase "I can see Russia from my house" whenever Palin's name pops up. It's not surprising that these imitations get noticed and talked about, given that these are known "characters" to people already based on the real-life individuals.

HOW YOU CAN CRAFT HUMOR THAT WORKS

I'm not going to lie to you, there is no magic potion or secret formula I can reveal that will make you a comic genius. The most importance piece of advice I can impart to you is, "get help from funny friends." Everybody has at least one funny friend, and probably a few. You don't necessarily need to find actual stand-up comics or writers, just find the people in your circle who are the ones that make you consistently laugh. Ask them for their help. Brainstorm with them.

And remember, your circle of friends should also include your friends on Facebook and other networks. Post a specific question and make it clear to people you're looking for funny responses or ideas. I've had tremendous success putting up questions on my feed, and asking for funny responses. For example, when lampooning an opposition candidate, I've asked the group to come up with "theme songs" or "running mates." Invariably, there's someone on the feed who comes up with a great idea. Usually, it gets even better after some back-and-forth riffing.

Have an idea or your own? A few? Go ahead and post those to your feed as well. See which ones generate the most responses, get the most "likes," and spur the most chatter.

Know Your Audience

As you craft your pitch, however, make sure to keep your target audience in mind. Will your humor appeal to them? If you have a specific demographic in mind (age, gender, location, etc.), is this something they will find particularly amusing? Something that speaks to them, feels particularly relevant, and such?

Remember, you're not just trying to come up with something funny for the sake of being funny, you're trying to craft a message that will spread among your target audience. For example, edgy, lewd jokes that might be perfectly appropriate for a younger edgier audience might fall completely flat among a more conservative or older audience. Likewise with the technology used to deliver your content. Email, for example, might be more appropriate for an older audience (or one that's a "newbie" audience for whatever reason), while Twitter might be more appropriate for a younger audience.

Of course, on the subject of lewd humor, don't assume even an older audience wants everything G-rated. Case in point, *Go the F*ck to Sleep* by Adam Mansbach, a tongue-in-cheek children's book, but aimed at parents dealing with children who wouldn't . . .

well, the title says it all. One might think parents would recoil at such obscenity. One would be wrong. The digital files of the galleys (the final versions for proofing, before printing) were spread around the Internet with such gusto (especially by parents) that it hit number one on Amazon—*before a single copy had been printed.*

Make Sure Your Message Is Along for the Ride

If something is forwarded to zillions of people, that's nice. But if the only thing they have in common is a love of humor, and they're not really your target audience, and your pitch isn't included (at least surreptitiously) as part of the pass-along, then what's the point?

What you're really looking for in this case is not just something funny, but something that is funny *and* can act as the "host mechanism" for the viral spreading of your message. Think again about your favorite funny TV ads. Are there any where you can remember the joke, but can't actually remember the brand being advertised? That's a perfect example of humor that was funny but not effective.

TACTICAL TIPS AND TRICKS

Although funny falls in the category of "I know it when I see it," and although there is no magic formula for guaranteeing success, there are definitely tips and tricks that I've found useful over the years for increasing the odds of something being funny, and in particular, for creating humor of the spreadable variety.

Get Punny

A good pun may seem like a groaner, but it's very memorable. It creates cognitive dissonance for just long enough to pierce through the cacophony of stimuli, and be memorable. Particularly effective is taking well-known names, clichés, words, or phrases, and coming up with rhymes or tweaks on them.

JustSayBlow.com, for example, was a campaign I ran against an antidrug politician (George W. Bush) who conveniently ignored his own past use of cocaine. Playing off the "just say no" drug war tagline, but using the slang term for cocaine, it was instantly memorable and almost always got a laugh.

Planet of the Grapes is a wine shop in London. Lord of the Fries is a restaurant in Melbourne, Australia, specializing in burgers and fries. Seoul Food serves up Korean food in Cambridge, Massachusetts. Groaners? For sure. But I'm willing to bet you're far more likely to remember *and spread* the names than if they'd simply been London Wine, Melbourne Burgers, and Cambridge Korean Restaurant.

Have Funny People Write It

Everyone would like to think they can do comedy. Not everyone can. If you're working as part of a company or group effort, you may need to fight this battle. Everyone wants to be part of the creative process when it comes to comedy. Resist. Get the help of truly funny people.

Don't Do Humor by Committee

Humor by committee never works. Too many cooks in the kitchen almost always leads to least common denominator output that is acceptable to all, but funny to none. If you find yourself brainstorming in a room with three or four funny people, great! If you find yourself in a room with nine or ten people, many of whom are "humor challenged," then politely excuse yourself, leave the room, and keep walking until you get somewhere far away, where they can never find you.

Try a Humor "Wind-Tunnel" Brainstorm

Some of the best, most clever stuff comes when you let your guard down, stop censoring yourself, and allow your subconscious funny guy to operate. Trying to come up with ideas to start? I'm a fan of the "Wind Tunnel" brainstorm technique described by Tim Hurson in his book, *Think Better.* With this approach, you move so quickly that you don't have time to censor yourself.

Force yourself to sit down with a voice recorder or pen and paper, and spit out ideas in a rapid-fire fashion. Whatever comes to mind, until you have fifty ideas. *Don't stop.* The first ten will be nonsense. The middle thirty will be reasonable, but odds are you'll find a gem or two among the final ten. No kidding. It really works.

Using Video? Keep It Short

A one-minute video is a lot longer than it sounds, especially when you're watching it on a computer monitor (even a big one). A few minutes is fine, but any more than that will be too long. And don't make it too overproduced. Ironically, often the slicker a video looks, the less likely it is to spread, as it will be seen as "advertising" rather than "organic content." Overproduced equals not authentic equals just not as spreadable.

Immediate Reaction

Finally, whatever you produce, judge it by the immediate reaction. If you have to explain the humor, it's not going to work, even if it's really funny. Remember, you can't ride shotgun with every email and status update, providing an explanation. If it doesn't work right away, the odds of it getting through the din are slim. And if it doesn't get through the din, it won't spread.

shareretweetrepeatshareretweet
repeatshareretweetrepeatshare
retweetrepeatshareretweetrepea

TEN

Giving Them a Problem

"THE SQUEAKY WHEEL GETS THE GREASE"

In today's media-saturated world, people are being messaged from every direction, and the stimuli are flying at a fast and furious pace. According to one recent study, the average American is subjected to 12,183 marketing messages in a typical day—12,183!*

Okay, I made that part up. And the footnote actually goes to a Rickroll. But while it might have seemed high, it didn't seem *that* high, did it? It probably seemed plausible, based on your own experience, right? People are overwhelmed. Stimulation and messages are all around us, and it's incredibly hard to get people to pay attention. Sometimes, you need to get a little creative.

---

* See presentation at www.youtube.com/watch?v=FKscaLcO7ko.

"You Need to Give Your Audience . . . a Problem"

This is how advertising maven Colin Drummond phrased it when we were on a panel together, and he was with the hotshot ad firm Crispin Porter & Bogusky. At the time, it struck me as a very intriguing point, and an odd one to make in the context of selling a product to a customer. Creating a problem? Isn't that the exact opposite of what you want to do? Aren't you trying to solve a problem for them?

Drummond's point stuck in my head, even years later. His talk about creating a problem had frankly created a problem for me. A logical inconsistency with what I'd believed to be true. Which proved exactly what Drummond was saying. Out of all the messages from the conference, that was the one I remembered.

OVERCOMING INERTIA

The squeaky wheel gets the grease, and the problem gets noticed.

But getting your message noticed is just part of the challenge. Overcoming inertia is even tougher. Getting your target audience to switch a brand or try something new isn't a small thing. It can mean a big shift in established patterns of behavior, and a lot of discomfort.

Think of your own experience. When you buy toothpaste, deodorant, or shampoo, do you actually make a conscious choice each time, weighing new options, or just go with your established habit? If you are in fact a creature of habit, you're not alone. As Drummond points out, "People love patterns and routine and order. They like finding something and sticking to it because it comforts them, it's convenient, it's predictable. There is always a tension that is in the way of doing the new thing."[11]

Further, it's not just about patterns, it's about signaling. Brands and consumers interact within what Drummond calls a "theater of culture." By using a certain brand, you are aligning yourself with it. You are sending a signal about who you are. You are communicating a lot about yourself to others, via brand by association. You can think of a brand as somewhat akin to a sports team. Both the Yankees and Red Sox are baseball teams, and thus ostensibly offering the same "product." But good luck getting a fan of one to switch to rooting for the other. The fans aren't just consuming a product, they're sending a signal as to who they are, what they're like, and where their alignments lie on a range of other fronts.

Change is problematic. If you want to get noticed, and you want your target audience to deal with the problem of switching to your brand or idea, or otherwise changing their pattern of behavior to your advantage—you need to present them with a problem yourself.

THE NEW CREEPIER BURGER KING

McDonald's versus Burger King is a classic example of a choice where patterns get set in stone. Any burger lover who eats fast food on a regular basis has almost surely aligned themselves with one over the other. Thus, when Drummond's agency, Crispin, was hired by Burger King, the agency knew it had a challenge—and would need to create a problem.

Crispin launched a new TV ad series for the company, one featuring a king who was frankly a bit creepy. It was a deliberate tactic, however, and one used to differentiate the king from the very safe and comfortable clown, Ronald McDonald.

Granted, some people find *any* clown to be creepy. But for most, Ronald McDonald represents a warm, safe figure from youth. The new Burger King, on the other hand, was another matter. As Drummond described it, the image was adapted from a king who graced the entrance to an old amusement park. A king thought to be, once again . . . kind of creepy.

People were transfixed by the new, weird king. Some hated it. Some loved it. But they talked about it. A lot. A Google search for it ("Burger King" + creepy ad) yields over two million results. It made an impact and helped give Burger King a bit more "edginess credibility" among its younger target audience.

Now, in fairness, there has been furious debate about the campaign among marketing professionals. Burger King's sales did rise initially, but then fell later. Of course, that fall did come during a recession. My own take? I think the campaign, while initially brilliant, simply got less novel and problem-inducing as people saw it more. And thus, it became less effective.

SACRIFICING FRIENDS FOR BURGERS

Moving to the world of social media, one tactic of Crispin's effort that was unquestionably brilliant, from a spread-worthiness perspective, was the Whopper Sacrifice. For this campaign, Burger King offered people a free Whopper—if they "de-friended" ten friends on Facebook. Those new ex-friends would be notified that they'd been sacrificed. For a Whopper.

This effort was carried out for a fraction of the price of the TV ad, but it created incredible buzz. It was fresh, funny, creative, and edgy. It created a problem for users. They had to actively think about who to de-friend, and they had to deal with the fact that they would have to explain to the friend why they did it.

In the span of less than one week, 233,906 friends were removed by 82,771 Facebook users. And this was back in January 2009, when the Facebook community was a fraction of the size it is now.

The chatter was incredible. For every person who actually did it, countless more people were talking about doing it, about whether it was good or bad, funny or mean. And not only were they talking about it, they were doing it on one of the most viral platforms on the planet. Then it went to an even higher level—when Facebook shut it down.

If Facebook thought that would quietly put an end to things, it thought wrong. An entirely new round of buzz ensued, as users and pundits discussed whether the disabling was fair or unfair, and whether, as mega-influential technology blog *TechCrunch* put it, "Facebook blows a whopper of an opportunity":

Burger King, through their insanely creative advertising agency Crispin Porter + Bogusky . . . launches a Facebook application that encourages users to remove Facebook friends . . . 233,906 friends were removed by 82,771 people in less than a week. What a great example to show the Madison Avenue agencies on how a big brand can get real engagement from users . . . Did anyone talk to the sales department before pulling the trigger on this?[12]

Reasonable people could certainly argue whether Facebook's move was fair or unfair, smart or dumb. And in fact, they did argue—the whole time talking about the Whopper and Burger King. No doubt, a whole lot of the folks doing the talking were McDonald's customers. And some of them were doubtless reexamining their own brand preferences.

HOW YOU CAN CREATE A PROBLEM FOR YOUR AUDIENCE

You may not be sitting on millions of dollars for a TV ad campaign, but there are still steps you can take to create a problem—and get noticed and talked about—as part of your marketing campaign.

Punny Double Takes

First, think if there's anything you can do to create some cognitive dissonance, or more simply put, something that makes people do a mental double take. In particular, remember the power of puns.

If you're launching a site or Facebook page, for example, consider using a URL or page name that is a play on a well-known phrase, but with a little tweak. JustSayBlow.com, for example, a site described in Chapter 9, was a play on the antidrug catchphrase, "Just say no." When people heard the URL, they would initially process it as JustSayNo.com, even before they finished reading it. After all, they'd heard "Just say no" so many times before, their mind was ready to fill in the blank. When they got to the last part, however, the mental double take set in. For a moment, there was the discomfort of the unexpected, followed by curiosity, followed by actual interest and attention.

ActForLove.org, the dating site for activists? It was this close to being called PeaceOfAss.org. Cooler, saner heads prevailed, but we have used this "naughty pun" technique for a number of Act-ForLove.org efforts. A voter registration effort, for example, was called "Shag the Vote," a play on "Rock the Vote." An effort targeting Canadians was our "Oh, oh, *oh, Canada*" campaign, a play on the Canadian national anthem. Sophomoric, yes, and that was part of their appeal. But by tweaking well-known familiar phrases, they also created a problem—a millisecond of "Wait, what?" That's enough to get noticed, and getting noticed is a start.

Remember the puns mentioned in Chapter 9? The Planet of the Grapes wine shop? The Lord of the Fries burger place? The Seoul Food Korean restaurant? None of those punny hooks took a million-dollar marketing budget—just some good creative brainstorming. Challenge yourself to do the same.

Screw Up

Make a mistake—deliberately. If you're placing an ad, do something out of the ordinary. When running ads with images, for example, I've occasionally put in the picture upside down. Other times, I've deliberately put in a misspelling. Invariably, it spurs smug emails from folks, pointing out the mistake. But it also invariably drives up the response. Remember, one click in a thousand views is a pretty decent response rate on Facebook. So if you can get even one in a hundred to notice an ad because of a weird twist, well . . . if even half of them proceed to click, you've just quintupled that "decent" response rate.

Moreover, people love to *spread* mistakes. The Internet is chock full of people who seem to revel in schadenfreude ("pleasure derived from the misfortune of others") and who apparently feel smarter when they can crow about someone else's error. Use this to your advantage. If one teeny mistake gets them to spread the 99 percent of your message that *is* correct, you've come out ahead.

Be Offensive

There's nothing like being offensive to create a problem for your audience. Offensive content gets noticed, gets a reaction, and gets spread. Now, you do need to straddle the line and not go too far. You wouldn't want to offend *all* your target audience, right? But what about offending half? Well, what if the content was so spread-worthy that ten times as many people saw it in the first place? Suddenly "half" of ten times as many people sounds pretty good, right?

One of the most iconic magazine covers of all time was for the first issue of *National Lampoon* magazine, in 1973. It featured a picture of a dog, with a hand holding a gun to its head, and the caption, "If you don't buy this magazine, we'll kill this dog." You can just imagine how that went over with animal lovers. It was offensive, it was shocking, and it was incredibly memorable. People talked about it like crazy, and four decades later, it's still all over the Internet. There's a reason why the American Society of Magazine Editors named it the seventh best cover of the last forty years.

Ashley Madison (AshleyMadison.com) is an online dating site. Launched in 2002, the site offered pretty much the same service as a zillion other dating sites that preceded it—the chance to post a profile, search for profiles posted by others, and see if you could find a match. What really differentiated the site, however, was its slogan: "Life Is Short. Have an Affair." Ashley Madison was unabashedly marketing infidelity. People were shocked. They were offended. But they were also curious and couldn't resist taking a peek. And they talked about it, and talked about it, and talked about it. *Time*, *Businessweek*, *Maxim*, *Sports Illustrated*, and a slew of other places covered it. Huge, huge swaths of people were offended by it—*and nine million others joined it*.

Now, granted, Ashley Madison didn't just have a slogan, they had a whole marketing effort. But the slogan was what differentiated it in a big way, and what turbocharged that effort—and you don't need a fortune to come up with a slogan.

Trying to figure out how to be offensive? Consider obscenities, or at least words that make people uncomfortable. Remember *Go the F*ck to Sleep*, the faux children's book mentioned in Chapter 9? No doubt, the title offended a whole lot of people, but in doing so it got their attention (while concurrently amusing a whole lot more people with its wonderful naughtiness). Ever heard of the play *The Vagina Monologues*? There's nearly two million hits for it on Google, so a whole lot of you have not only heard about it, but talked about it as well. If it had been titled something a bit less risqué (*Monologues From the Heart* or whatever), it would have gotten far less attention. It's hard to hear that title and not be a little jolted.

In my own experience, I've taken a lot of flak for a few of my edgy Facebook page titles. "Telling Sarah Palin She's Full of Crap," for example, has elicited a number of angry emails, from Republicans and Democrats alike, who feel the "crap" part is inappropriate. On the other hand, it's also generated over one hundred thousand fans with no marketing budget whatsoever— something I'm confident would not have happened if it had been named "Telling Sarah Palin She's Lying."

Now, needless to say, you'll need to be careful here. You don't want to take it so far that you're disgusting or profoundly offending your target audience. You'll need to gauge the limits based on your situation and target audience, but certain areas are clearly over the line. Racism, sexism, and homophobia, for example, are places you really just shouldn't go. Ditto with anything really scatological. You want to offend them a bit—not repulse them outright.

IT MAY SOUND CRAZY TO try to reach your target audience by striving to create a problem for them. But if the alternative is being ignored, then "crazy" might be your most sane approach.

ELEVEN

Using Sex Appeal

"LOVE MAKES THE WORLD GO AROUND"

Sex, love, romance—it sells. And it spreads. And it's something you should at least consider taking advantage of if you want to get the most out of your marketing efforts.

We've gone to the moon, we've split the atom, and we've even managed to create cola with zero calories. Impressive stuff, to be sure, but don't let yourself be fooled. At our core, human beings are just well-dressed monkeys.

We like to pretend we've evolved, but human beings remain remarkably motivated by the things that motivated our primate ancestors—food, shelter, and yes, sex. You may be recoiling at this point, insisting that a higher-minded approach is surely preferable. Before you go that route, however, consider the following statistics:

- A Google search for "food" yields 1.4 billion results. A Google search for "sex" yields over 2 billion. Love? More than 3 billion.

- The website for the magazine *GQ* typically gets 2.5 million views a week, with viewers drawn by a range of quality editorial content focusing on fashion and social commentary. The week it featured a scantily clad photo spread of the attractive young stars of the TV show *Glee*, it received 33 million views.[13]

- On Facebook, as of early 2011, the page for NPR had 1.5 million fans, and the *Wall Street Journal* had over 200,000. Clearly a sign that people are drawn to high-quality, intellectual content, right? Well, not quite as impressive when you consider that at the same point in time ridiculously hot actress Megan Fox had 23 million, and equally ridiculously hot musician Shakira had 28 million (not to downplay their talent at all, but looking at the pictures they've chosen to feature on their Facebook pages, it's pretty clear they understand the added value of being scandalously attractive).

The point isn't that people *can't* think at a level higher than a chimp, it's simply that base needs and desires are *extraordinarily powerful*. Far more powerful than we often are willing to admit, particularly in a meeting with clients or colleagues. It's rather awkward to say, "Yes, it's nice and quaint that you have all these ideas about ways to make an intellectual argument to your target audience, but they actually care more about scantily clad models." Even admitting this to yourself is hard enough.

But let's assume you were able to gather all 500 of the Fortune 500 CEOs in one room. And let's say you could ask them the following question: "How many of you thought in the last hour about new ways to increase your company's sales?" Followed by another question: "During that same hour, how many of you thought about sex?" The first question might be critical to their corporation's well-being, and yet . . . the reality is, more hands would probably go up for the second one.

There's no use denying it. It's hardwired. Moreover, people

don't think about sex, they talk about sex. And love, romance, and all iterations of it. They make jokes about it. They ask for advice. They talk about celebrities they think are hot. It's an eminently spread-worthy topic.

Don't believe me? Consider the case of HotOrNot.com. Founded in 2000, it began as a site that consisted of nothing more than a series of pictures, uploaded by users themselves, and rateable by other users on a scale of one to ten. Basically, users just sat there, clicking one through ten for each picture, and then rating the next one . . . and the next one, and the next one. The site would then display an average of the ratings for each photo. Within a week of launching, it reached nearly two million page views per day, all through word-of-mouth spreading. *In one week. With no marketing budget.* Oh, and this basic, bare-bones site? It ended up selling for a reported purchase price of *$20 million.*[14]

Remember the story from Chapter 1 about the 2008 videos on behalf of then Senator Obama? Remember the "Crush on Obama" one from "Obama Girl," pining away about her crush on the presidential candidate? The video received tens of millions of views, and anyone who's seen it knows that a lot of those were undoubtedly views and reviews by people with their own crushes on Obama Girl, the smoking-hot Amber Lee Ettinger. It was a funny, clever video, but picture it with any of the "5s" from HotOrNot.com, and it's hard to see it igniting such a firestorm.

MARKETING TO OUR INNER MONKEY

So what to make of this? Am I suggesting you jettison your current offerings and instead dive into the lucrative world of porn? Strip down to a bikini or Speedo for all of your photo and video shoots?

Hardly. It's simply a suggestion to not rule out sex appeal and instead to keep in mind its potential power as you craft content and lay out a plan. Ideally, at least test it to see the reaction. And if the data shows you that being sexy is the way to be smart, then go with it.

You may feel a bit cheesy appealing to people's animal instincts, but if that's what works, that's what works. Stop feeling guilty. It's not your fault that a few million years of lizard brain instinct have hardwired into us drivers that we haven't "unwired" in a few thousand years of (alleged) civilization.

Use Hot People

Sorry, I just can't sugarcoat it. If you're putting up a Facebook ad, for example, the reality is that a picture of a hot person will simply get more attention and more clicks. Selling cars? Use a hot person. Selling sports equipment? Use a hot person. Selling accounting services? You get the idea. Of course you'll want to test, but the hot image is going to work better.

Now, before you send me angry emails, remember, I'm not suggesting what should be, but simply what has been shown time and time again to be more effective. I have consistently doubled or tripled the response rate to an ad by using a picture of a hot person as opposed to . . . well, someone who looks like me!

Incorporate Animal Instincts into Your Business Model

I have been helping organize on the activism front for years, but one of my best efforts in terms of return on investment was ActForLove.org, the dating site for activists mentioned earlier. Within a few weeks of launch, it was already far outstripping the site traffic of some of the best known national activist organizations. And for every one person visiting the activism part of the site, there were ten visitors to the personals section. As *Newsweek* reported about the site, "Finally, someone is being honest about the link between political activism and gettin' some action!"

You don't need a multimillion-dollar back-end platform to do this, however. Uptown Valet is a dry cleaner in the Georgetown neighborhood of Washington, DC. When you walk in, you notice something different about it—it's also a matchmaking center. There are Polaroid snapshots of dozens of customers adorning one of the walls, along with Post-it messages from other customers who liked what they saw. It's fun, friendly, and not the least bit sleazy—and there's no doubt that at least some of the regular customers picked Uptown over the many other nearby competitors for this very reason.

Sometimes, you don't even need a shop. Ahmed Ibrahim is a New York City taxi driver who actually runs a blind dating service from his cab. He simply takes numbers from interested passengers and calls them when he meets other interested passengers who seem like good matches. Since 2004, he's set up over a hundred couples, with nearly thirty of these leading to relationships.[15] Plus, he's generated enormous chatter and earned media coverage from a slew of organizations, ranging from MSNBC to the *Wall Street Journal.*

Use Sex Appeal as a Lure

PETA (People for the Ethical Treatment of Animals) is an animal rights organization that has gained an enormous amount of traction by incorporating sex appeal into its marketing. Its advertisements are highly suggestive, with some even including outright nudity. On the online front, each year it puts out a video parodying the presidential state of the union address—but with the address given by a very attractive woman who strips during the course of it. While doing so, she also recites key PETA message points, such as opposing cruelty to animals or promoting the advantages of veganism. Every year, the videos generate an astonishing amount of views. While most undoubtedly come for the nudity, at least some leave with a better appreciation for the message and an intention to change their own behavior. This use of sex appeal is of course *highly* controversial and has earned PETA many detractors. But it has also earned it over a million Facebook fans and website traffic that far outstrips that of competing organizations.

AGAIN, THIS IS NOT TO say that using sex is the *only* way to go—just that it's often overlooked because people feel weird about it and rule it out, as opposed to actually doing a real assessment of its effectiveness. Of course, you might not want to go that route, preferring to give up some effectiveness in the name of principle. And in some cases, your audience may truly be different and more attuned to a cerebral pitch. That's cool. Just be honest with yourself and make sure you recognize the trade-off, and are not pretending a more high-minded choice is truly optimal when it isn't.

TWELVE

Testing Your Message for Effectiveness

TAKE YOUR BEST SHOT, BUT THEN TEST, TEST, TEST

Okay, let's assume that you've got your message crafted. A wonderful one, using the lessons learned in earlier chapters. Ready, aim, fire? Not quite. Before hitting your "fire away" button, don't forget to test.

TESTING YOUR EMAIL MESSAGE

Let's start with email. First, a caveat—this process requires taking small samples for testing purposes, just a few percent of your list. Thus, realistically, if your list is on the small side, a few hundred or less, this probably won't yield statistically significant data for comparison.

Okay, caveat aside, here's how you should proceed.

Step 1: Separate Your List into a Few Test Groups

I like to use at least three groups, each with 3 to 5 percent of the list. Each group should be the same size, and have a critical mass of at least a hundred (and ideally a few hundred) emails in order to get good data. If your list is smaller, take a higher percentage.

Try to make these groups as randomly chosen as possible. Many email systems will let you do this automatically. Short of that, try separating into groups based on something close to random, such as the first letter of their email address or name.

Step 2: Craft Your Subject Line

If your subject line isn't interesting enough to make the recipient want to open the email, the message can't get acted upon, so this is critical. Come up with your three best, and set up three emails to go with those subject lines. To keep things straight, let's call them subject lines 1, 2, and 3.

For example, let's say you're sending an email newsletter for your wine shop, and you've got three stories to tell: (1) You're having a wine tasting next Tuesday; (2) you're having a sale on Italian wines; (3) you're starting a new "wine lovers" dating service in the store, à la the one done by the dry cleaner in Chapter 11.

The simplest test would be to highlight a different one of the three stories in the three different subject lines:

1. **Wine tasting next Tuesday**

2. **Sale on Italian wines**

3. **"Wine lovers" matchmaking service**

Alternatively, if you were just focusing on one story, you might want to test things like tone (funny versus serious), clarity (straightforward versus mysterious) or any number of other attributes. For now, however, since the point here is to explain how to test, let's keep it simple and use the subject lines above.

Step 3: Craft Three Different Versions of Your Email Body Text

Let's call them email bodies A, B, and C. They don't have to be radically different; slight modifications are fine. Try playing around with the language, the order of the items, and the images. Make sure to set them up in such a way that you can judge which was most successful.

Continuing with the wine shop example, you've got three stories, so one approach would simply be to have three different emails with one story prioritized in each one. If you were writing a three-hundred-word email, for example, you could have two hundred words on the prioritized story, and fifty-word snippets on the other two. Alternatively, you could try different tones—comedic versus serious, for example, or different images. Over the course of weeks or months, you might want to try testing all of these things.

Let's say, however, that we wanted to test email length. Our three emails might consist of a fifty-word teaser, a one-hundred-fifty-word set of blurbs, or a three-hundred-word more explanatory version. Leaving aside formatting and imagery for now, here's how the body text of your three emails might be scripted:

EMAIL A: 50-WORD SHORT VERSION

Dear XX:

Thank you for supporting Mario's Wine Shop! There's lots happening this week, so make sure to stop by! (1) A wine tasting next Tuesday; (2) a sale on Italian wines; and (3) a new "wine lovers" matchmaking service!

Click here to visit our website and learn more.

EMAIL B: 150-WORD MEDIUM VERSION

Dear XX:

Thank you for supporting Mario's Wine Shop, a neighborhood favorite for over twenty-five years.

There's lots happening this week, so make sure to stop by!

- Wine tasting next Tuesday: We'll be tasting some wonderful red wines next Tuesday, from 5 to 6 p.m. As a regular customer, you're welcome to participate for free. Click to learn more!

- Sale on Italian wines: Love Italian wines? Here's your chance to get some wonderful ones for 25 percent off our already low prices! Click to learn more!

- New "wine lovers" matchmaking service: Are you single, and looking to meet a fellow wine lover? Then our new "wine lovers" matchmaking service is for you! Click to learn more!

We hope to see you this week, and hope you can join in the fun. Need directions or more information? Click here to visit our website.

EMAIL C: 300-WORD LONG VERSION

Dear XX:

Thank you for supporting Mario's Wine Shop, a neighborhood favorite for over twenty-five years. We're delighted to have you as a customer!

There's lots happening this week, so make sure to stop by!

Wine tasting next Tuesday: We'll be tasting some wonderful wines next Tuesday, from 5 to 6 p.m. We'll start off with some wonderful white wines, including some brand-new French varieties, then move on to some lovely reds, and finish off with some unbeatable dessert wines. As a regular customer, you're welcome to participate for free. Click to learn more!

Sale on Italian wines: Love Italian wines? Here's your chance to get some wonderful ones for 25 percent off our already low prices! We'll be celebrating Columbus Day with a tribute to Italy, and a sale on Chianti, Pinot Grigio, Frascati, and a range of others. Click to learn more!

New "wine lovers" matchmaking service: Are you single, and looking to meet a fellow wine lover? Then our new "wine lovers" matchmaking service is for you! Have fun and meet other wine lovers in the comfort of our friendly wine shop. The process is simple—we take a picture of you, put it up on our wall, and if other singles find you interesting, they can leave a note for you. If you make a connection, we'll even give you a free bottle of wine for your first date. Click to learn more!

We hope to see you this week, and hope you can join in the fun. Need directions or more information? <u>Click here</u> to visit our website. And remember, good news—like good wine—is meant to be shared. So please share this email with your friends and family!

For now, don't get hung up on the specific text in these samples, just note how they convey the same information in different lengths. Also note how each includes multiple links back to the website. Your goal may be to actually get them to visit the store, of course, but you'll need to be able to measure some more tangible proxy to judge success on that front. More simply put, if one email gets twice as many clicks, it doesn't guarantee that twice as many people will come to the store, but if you had to bet your life on which one would lead to more visits, that would be a pretty good one to go with.

In order to measure relative effectiveness of the different emails, you'll need a way to track which visits came from which email. Most email programs should be able to tell you how many clicks a link got, and that's a good start. You should also supplement this with statistics on the site end as well, ones that measure page views generated. The precise approach for this will depend on which system you're using to host your site. Typically, however, you would add a suffix to the end of a URL, such as "?email1," as in "MariosWineShop.com?email1." It would still take a clicker to the same page, but the part after the "?" would be captured by the site and associated with that record. If you don't have this as part of your system, you could also create three cloned pages. It's a little more of a pain, but does the trick.

Step 4: Mix and Match

Now match up the subject headers and email text, so you have three individual emails, each with a different subject and each with different text. Let's call these emails 1A, 2B, and 3C. Then fire away to the three test groups, and wait for the results. If you can wait a day for data, that's great. But if not, even a few hours should start to give you a reasonably reliable picture. But remember, viral spreading takes time, and it's virality that we're trying to measure. So ideally give it at least a day or two to happen. If recipients haven't spread it by then, the odds they'll ever do it are slim.

Step 5: Judgment Time!

First, the subject line. Look at the *open* rates. Whichever email has the best *open* rate is the winning *subject* line. Open rate is something that any decent email system should be able to tell you.

Next, to judge the winning email body text, look and see which email generated the most site visits as a percentage of opens. That is, make sure to adjust for the quality of the subject line. If all the emails had the exact same open rate, then the email that provoked the most clicks is the "winner" when it comes to body text. However, if 1A had four times the open rate as 2B, but 2B generated half as many site visits, then B is the winning email.

Note: In this example, we've looked specifically at site visits as the measure of success. Depending on your situation and goals, however, you might want to look at other measures. If you were marketing a book online, for example, and sales was your sole measure of success (and you could measure it), you would want to judge the winning email on that basis instead.

Step 6: Send the Winner

Match up the winning subject line and winning email, and get ready to hit send. So if subject line 1 had the highest open rate, for example, but email text C had the highest success rate, then 1C is your winning combination.

When you're done, take some time to really think through the data, process what you learned from it, and use it to help refine your next round of messaging.

Seem like a lot of work? Indeed it is. But if you've got tens of thousands, hundreds of thousands, or even more emails, small differences in response rates can mean a heck of a difference in whether or not you're successful. In a list of one thousand, for example, getting a 20 percent click-through rate versus 15 percent means you just got fifty more clicks.

TESTING YOUR SOCIAL MEDIA MESSAGE

With social media, you don't really have the luxury of pretesting to small groups in the same way, at least not without a lot more hassle. But you still can compare effectiveness across different posts, see what works, and adjust your content accordingly moving forward.

For Twitter, this is relatively simple. Check each post to see whether it was mentioned or retweeted, and if so, how many times. This is information that Twitter links to right from your home page. This tells you virality. If you have a link in the text, you can of course also measure clicks to that as well.

For Facebook, it's a little trickier, but still quite doable. For effectiveness, you can of course measure clicks, if you're sending them to your own website. For virality, keep an eye on your posts and see how many "impressions" they get. Facebook shows this stat to admins, just below the post (there's sometimes a delay, and it doesn't always show up on smaller pages). Let's say you have ten thousand fans on a page, but the number of impressions is twenty thousand. That's a sign that there was some viral spreading. If, on the other hand, the next post had only five thousand impressions, that's a sign that it didn't have much virality, at least in comparison.

Now, it's part science and part art. For the art, it really means using your head. If one was posted at three p.m. and one at three a.m., take that into account. But overall, it isn't rocket science—eyeball the viralization rates, and do more of what seems to work. Then lather, rinse, repeat.

IN THE MONTHS AND YEARS to come, as these social media platforms hopefully open up more of their data, we may be able to move more from art to science. For now, however, though the data isn't perfect or perfectly accessible, even some minimal focus and thinking can make a big difference.

PART FOUR

ENGAGING THE RIGHT MESSENGERS

You've got the right content; you've got the right tools.

Now it's time to find the right messengers. In the age of the Internet, nearly anyone can spread a message, but not everyone does spread it. And fewer still spread successfully.

We've talked in general about these people, the multipliers, and what they're capable of. But now let's talk about how you actually find them.

This section will examine some of the key techniques for identifying multipliers and for honing your message to appeal to them in particular.

THIRTEEN

Finding the Multipliers

We know that the power of the individual to virally spread a message has expanded by leaps and bounds in the last several years. With a touch of a few keystrokes, the average Internet user could reach thousands in just a few minutes.

But while most *could*, only few actually *do*. And even fewer do it *effectively*. Those who do are the multipliers. The people who will literally multiply the message that you send to them. These people are at the heart of any effective viral campaign. Yes, you want that message to be as viral as possible. But you also want to target it toward the messengers that will actually viralize it to a large audience.

THE IMPORTANCE OF MULTIPLIERS

Regardless of what idea, product, or service you're hawking, the odds are good that there are multipliers willing to spread your message—if you can find them, and if you can give them the right message to spread.

No doubt, you've seen a version of multipliers described elsewhere. It's a concept that's made its way into the meme-osphere. In his book *Purple Cow*, Seth Godin discusses a concept very much akin to multipliers—"sneezers," those who are most apt to spread something virally. The same way literal sneezers spread an actual virus, these metaphorical sneezers spread new ideas through talking, email, telephone, and in-person conversation. They are the perceived authorities who tell their colleagues and friends about new ideas and products, and thus spread the virus.

Note: Whether one is a "perceived expert" can change, depending on the context. My friend Fred, for example, is a professional comedian, and one of the funniest guys I know. So funny, in fact, that he actually went on to become a star on *Saturday Night Live* (you read about him already in Chapter 9). My childhood friend Jason has always had a keen eye for numbers and finance and went on to become an extremely successful investment-fund manager.

Suffice to say, when Fred emails something he says is funny— I pay attention, as do a heck of a lot of other people. If a hundred people were cc'd on that email, you better believe that 90 percent would open and read it. And when Jason emails financial advice—I pay attention, as do a heck of a lot of other people. Again, a hundred people cc'd, ninety reads or better. But switch the subjects between the two, and they suddenly go from "influential" status to "regular friend" status.

Although it can be interesting and even helpful to try to identify "influentials in a vacuum," devoid of context, the reality is, you will only know whether someone will be an effective multiplier for your product once you are measuring their actions in that specific context, or at least in a context similar enough to provide useful data.

Finding Your Multipliers Through Email Activity

We've already covered email as a technology in Chapter 4 and as a tactic in Chapter 12. But let's look at how you can use email to identify who on your list is a multiplier.

Once you have your system in place, and you are ready to start sending emails, there are a number of stats you'll want to track. The basics include open rates, click-through rates, and success rates (whether your emails achieved your goals, whatever they might be). That's fairly standard for testing the effectiveness of an email. However, if you're looking for multipliers specifically, you'll need to dig more deeply and measure who is actually doing the spreading.

Who are the email recipients whose spreading is resulting in the most clicks? This will differ slightly, depending on how your email system tracks this. However, if an email system does track on an individual basis, it typically does so by creating a customized link for each recipient. For example, the link in your email wouldn't be "KatesAwesomeWine.com," it would be something like "KatesAwesomeWine.com/125836." The system can then track your click specifically to you. If you're on some email lists yourself, go and look at the last few emails you received, click on a few links, and you'll likely notice a whole slew of numbers and/or letters appearing after the actual URL of the page. That tells the email tracking system that it was the email received by you that generated that click.

For multiplier tracking purposes, you'll want to look for individual links that show up multiple times. For some systems, this process may be automated, but that's still rare (since what we're talking about here is still frankly on the cutting edge). For most you'll need to either set up a report or eyeball the logs (if you don't see an intuitive way to do it in your system, this would be a good time to splurge on a tech consultant. A good one should be able to set up a simple report for you in a few hours or less).

If you see a link showing up as having been clicked multiple times, it is very likely a sign that the individual who received the email with that link is a multiplier. If, for example, the link above showed up 138 times, it's possible that someone sat there clicking refresh over and over, but a lot more likely that that person forwarded the email (or posted it on a blog or site or somewhere with an audience) and the recipients respected that person enough to open it and click through themselves. Of course, it's also possible that the individual forwarded it just one time to *someone else* who forwarded it to 136 others. But if you see the same recipient showing up as a multiplier on email after email, it's a safe bet that they're the one doing the multiplying.

When it comes to multipliers, it's not uncommon to see a tiny percentage of a list doing the majority of the multiplying. At the extremes, it may literally be as high as 1 percent doing 99 percent of the spreading. With one effort, I was stunned to see a link show up as clicked over a thousand times. One individual had accounted for 99 percent of the spreading for that email! (It turns out it was a blogger who'd cut and pasted the email into a post on his mega high-traffic blog.)

Honing in on this tiny percentage will enable you to follow up with customized outreach that simply would not be possible for the full list. Let's say you had a list of ten thousand people. Crafting an individualized thank-you email to each and every one of them would take weeks. But if you knew that 1 percent of them— one hundred people—were doing 99 percent of the spreading, that would be a whole lot easier. It might just take a few hours. In my experience, even a simple email that is clearly personalized can really make an impact. Beyond that, you might want to offer them special VIP perks. In the wine-shop-tasting example from Chapter 12, you could offer invites solely to multipliers. If you were selling a new poetry book, perhaps you'd want to thank them with an autographed copy. Hey, if they spread the word so effectively, that one copy given away will probably lead to a few actual sales from their friends.

Now, one note to keep in mind. When you do reach out to

these folks, you might want to hold off on saying something as specific as "Say, we've been tracking your links and your spreading, and making meticulous notes about what you're doing . . ." Most Internet users are smart enough to realize that tracking occurs, but you don't want to sound creepy or Orwellian. Just let them know you appreciate all the work they're doing as a "top supporter" and leave it at that. If they ask, it's certainly fine to tell them the details, I'd just be wary of leading with it before you've established a rapport.

FINDING YOUR MULTIPLIERS THROUGH SOCIAL MEDIA ACTIVITY

The mere fact that someone is active on Facebook, Twitter, and other platforms doesn't *guarantee* they're a multiplier, or that they'll multiply for you. But all else being equal, who do you think would be a more likely multiplier:

- Bill, with an email list of five hundred, who avoids social media.

- Ted, with an email list of five hundred, who also has a thousand Facebook friends and a thousand Twitter followers.

Yes, we can all think of exceptions to the rule and extraordinary cases. But it doesn't take a rocket scientist to guess that Ted would be more likely to be a multiplier. Ted starts off with an audience five times the size as Bill's. Plus, the fact that he's proactively chosen to engage in the highly exhibitionist/voyeuristic world of social media speaks volumes.

For this reason, it's very much in your interest to learn who among your supporters are members of social media communities and to focus your message on what appeals to them. Assuming you're starting with a good email list, you can run a social media scan on it that identifies who on the list is a member of Facebook, Twitter, and other key social media communities. Rapleaf (Rapleaf

.com), a Silicon Valley firm, is the leader among those offering this type of service. For a reasonable fee, Rapleaf will take your email list, scan it, and return it to you with social media memberships appended. That is, where before it might have said "John Hlinko = John@ShareRetweetRepeat.com," it will now include entries indicating the member is on Facebook, MySpace, Twitter, and a range of other platforms, as well as a trove of other information that Rapleaf has accumulated through years of searches of public information.

If you are on a tight budget and want to go with a scaled-down, free version of this, both Facebook and Twitter have "find friends" features that allow you to upload your email list to see who is on those services (see "friend finder" on Facebook and "who to follow" on Twitter). In both cases, the way it works is pretty much the same. You allow Facebook or Twitter to scan your email contact list, and then it spits out a page with who is on that service already. The downside is that you don't get as much information as Rapleaf, and also that you'll need to upload your list to a personal email service first (AOL, Gmail, Yahoo!, etc.) and add them as contacts for it to work. If you have a large list, you hit size limitations that require you to create a separate personal email account. Still though, this option is free, and it's a great way to start.

Tracking Social Media Spreading in Action

Beyond analyzing the size of an individual's potential social-media audience, you can also track actual sharing in action. It takes a bit more work (that is, it's less automatable than email tracking), but is still quite doable unless your following is truly massive.

On Twitter, this is relatively straightforward. When you post an update, check back in a few hours or even a few days to see who's been sharing and retweeting it. On your main Twitter dashboard, you can click on "retweets" to see who's retweeted your post, and "@mentions" to see who's mentioned you (literally who has included your Twitter name with the "@" before it, something customary since it then creates an automatic hyperlink back to your page). You can also do a search for your name in the search box, something that will surface mentions that didn't include the "@." When you find folks retweeting or mentioning you in a positive way, consider sending them a "thanks" message or responding to their tweet with your own. Something as simple as "Thanks for the RT! @TheirName" is a nice way for them to feel appreciated (and the "@TheirName" part ensures that your tweet will show up in their searches when they look to see who's talking about them). A small sign of thanks like this can go a long way. Remember, if they're retweeting or mentioning you, they clearly value what you have to say.

Keep an eye out for "retweeter repeaters," folks who retweet your messages on a regular basis. As with the email example cited earlier, consider reaching out to these proven multipliers and offering them special perks. Pay special attention to people who have a lot of followers, something you can see when you click over to their page. Also, since Twitter feeds are public (unlike email), you might want to take advantage of that fact, and scan their tweets before reaching out to them. Basically, you'll just want to make sure they're not crazy before engaging them.

With Facebook, monitoring sharing is a little trickier, but still quite doable. Using the Facebook search box, simply type in the name of your page, and see who has mentioned it in their posts. Make sure to click on the option "posts by everyone" so you see who has mentioned it above and beyond just your own personal base of friends.

You can also find mentions by looking for people who click "share" when you post a link. This is where the trickier part comes in. Note that when you post a link on your page, Facebook includes a title for the link. Typically, it pulls that in from the page whose link you included, but you can also change it yourself. If you put in "ESPN.com," for example, Facebook automatically includes the title "ESPN: The Worldwide Leader in Sports." If you put in a link to an article, it typically pulls in the headline.

To see who has shared your link, type in the title (not the URL) into the Facebook search box, and again, search for "posts by everyone." For example, if you linked to an article on your blog, and the title was "Greatest wines under $10," typing that title into the search box would show you who had shared that post. Note: If you're posting something on Facebook, and the title automatically pulled in is something incredibly generic, such as "news," make sure to tweak the title to something more distinct. Otherwise, finding your shares in a sea of look-alikes will be much harder.

Again, when you see sharers, consider sending them a thank-you message. When you find the repeat sharers, consider offering special perks. And remember, as with Twitter, keep a special eye out for those with a lot of friends and a wary eye out for those whose posts on their page indicate they might be not quite sane.

THE "MEGA MULTIPLIERS"

Even if 1 percent of your list is doing 99 percent of the multiplying, there's a chance that there is another segment within that 1 percent that is multiplying at an even higher level. These are the "mega multipliers." In a list of thousands they may be the few dozen, or even just the *few* who are driving incredible numbers of people your way. They may be the people with enormous email lists, highly trafficked blogs, or Facebook or Twitter followings in the tens or hundreds of thousands, or higher. They may be reporters or columnists with a national following. They may be celebrities. Or they may simply be incredibly influential for some other reason.

If you are fortunate enough to come across these folks among your supporters, you should of course use the same techniques described earlier to engage them. But you may want to take it even a step higher. First, if you don't recognize their name, use the web to learn who they are. Google them, and look for them on LinkedIn and on Facebook. It's important for you to know who you're resonating with, and by searching, you might find a real diamond. In one online marketing effort I led, we did a little research on a particularly enthusiastic follower—and discovered he was one of the top directors in Hollywood. I hadn't recognized the name initially, but when I saw the movies he had directed, I knew every single one (including some huge blockbusters).

You may find that multiplying online is just the start of what they can do. You may get incredibly lucky and find a celebrity who can promote your cause on TV, or a wealthy benefactor who can help support your cause. Crazier things have happened, and if you get lucky and do some digging, something wonderfully crazy might happen to you.

FINDING AND ENGAGING MULTIPLIERS TAKES WORK, and is part science and part art. But it is the multipliers that are at the heart of any effective viral campaign. Ultimately, it is people who spread messages. Finding the right ones and effectively engaging them is absolutely key to making your viral campaign all it can be, and the work to do so is almost always time well spent.

FOURTEEN

Skewing Your Strategy to Multipliers

Once you've identified your multipliers, it's time for the after-action work—the work necessary to best delineate and serve your multipliers. You'll want to do three things: (1) Update your records noting who is and who isn't a multiplier; (2) determine which message resonated best with the multipliers; and (3) start to skew your strategy accordingly.

UPDATING YOUR RECORDS

On the email front, figure out which members of your list have multiplied the most—that is, those who have provoked the most clicks (or some other measure of success, such as sales, if appropriate to your situation). Enter that information into your database or email system in some way that you can later track and reach out to just this group.

Most systems will allow you to add a "custom" field (or group), which is simply a fancy way of keeping track of some variable that isn't standard (name, address, email, etc.). In this case, I typically opt for the simple path of adding a field called "multiplier." If any individual proves him or herself to be one, I put in a "yes." This enables tracking of performance by these folks as a group, and also allows for things like sending emails just to them and no one else (special invites, for example).

For Twitter multipliers, you can create a Twitter "list" and add their names. Twitter allows you to do this from the home page fairly easily, and it's a fairly simply way of keeping track of them. With Facebook, there's not currently a similarly easy way to track fans. You can create lists within your personal account to track your friends, but unfortunately there's not a good way for a fan page to do that to track fans. For now, at least, your best bet is to simply keep a list of them in a separate file (Word, Excel, Google Doc, or whatever you prefer).

TRACKING MULTIPLIERS ACROSS PLATFORMS

Next, it's time to get a little fancier: take your Facebook and Twitter multipliers, look to see if they are in your email database, and then update that database as well. It might be that someone is regularly sharing your messages on Facebook and Twitter, but not email. But the bottom line is that they're still multiplying your messages, and that's worth keeping track of. Further, because you can control your email database and manipulate and analyze the data (as opposed to Facebook or Twitter, where those companies control the data), it's the logical place to have as your main database for ongoing analysis. If you wanted, for example, to know what cities your top one hundred Facebook multipliers were from, you could always scroll through their profiles one by one and probably knock it out in an hour or so. But if that information were in a real database where you could run a query, it'd take no more than a few seconds.

On the flip side, you should also track who among your email multipliers is on Twitter and Facebook and update those lists as well. Given how naturally viral those platforms are, it's to your advantage to entice email multipliers to take their viralizing ways to the world of social media too. This may be as simple as a custom email to that group, explaining how sharing works on Twitter and Facebook. You'd be surprised how many people, even ones with large followings, simply aren't familiar with how to retweet or share something on Facebook (especially the latter, since Facebook has tweaked the process multiple times).

Update Your Data

Once you've recorded the data and tracked your multipliers accordingly, make sure to update this data regularly. Each time someone spreads a message, add them into the multiplier category.

In general, I'd recommend not removing people from the list, unless they've really become nonresponsive altogether for a long time (say, six months or more). Remember, multipliers will likely not multiply every single message. Some will resonate with them, and some will not. You're just looking for people with the *capability* and *willingness* to multiply, not the *certainty*.

SKEWING YOUR MESSAGE TO MULTIPLIERS

Let's flash forward a few weeks. Let's say you've sent a few messages and have enough information to track your top multipliers. You know who the ones are who have the capability to spread a message, even if they don't do it every time.

It's time to start focusing your message on these people in particular. Keep track of what messages and types of themes or calls to actions are actually causing them to multiply. And then start moving more and more in that direction with subsequent communications.

For example, let's return to the wine shop email from Chapter 12, the one where we were deciding whether to promote (via the subject line) a wine tasting event, a sale on Italian wines, or a new "wine lovers" matchmaking service. Now, you already know from that chapter how to test different versions of a single email for impact, effectiveness, and virality. And in fact, because the ones spreading the email are themselves the multipliers, what is effective virally is most likely what is most effective for the multipliers specifically as well.

Let's take it from one email to several emails over the course of several weeks. For simplicity's sake, assume that you were testing the same three broad subjects each time. Let's say that in each case, the tasting event version performed slightly better overall, but that you noticed that the multipliers themselves were consistently opening the wine sale version at a much higher rate. What this might tell you is that although the wine tasting was proving more viral thus far, the wine sale email might have more potential virality. That is, if it's doing the best job of catching the interest of the multipliers, your challenge might simply be figuring out a way to make the wine sale message itself more viral.

To clarify, let's look at an extreme version of this. Assume that your wine shop email list could be broken down into two groups. Group A members each had ten email contacts. Group B members each had ten *million* email contacts. If the wine tasting emails performed better overall, that would be meaningful. But if the Group B members were opening the wine sale emails at a far higher rate, that would be a powerful sign that if you could make those emails more spread-worthy, your *potential* rewards could be astronomically higher.

LOOK FOR TRENDS AND ADJUST YOUR MARKETING ACCORDINGLY

As you continue with your campaign, try to accumulate as much demographic data as you can on the multipliers. Age, gender, geographic location—whatever you can find, make sure to enter it in your database, and then look for trends. Are they more likely to be men? Women? Old or young? From a specific geographic area?

If you start to see definite trends emerging, you may want to consider shifting your marketing effort accordingly. Let's say you were selling your new poetry book, and you were targeting your advertising toward twentysomething women in San Francisco, figuring, not unreasonably, that it was a demographic more likely to like poetry. But then you noticed a trend among your multipliers—they were overwhelmingly fortysomething men in North Dakota. What could explain this? Well, many things, but frankly, who cares? Maybe it's something in the water, the milk, or the waving wheat, but if your goal is to maximize viral spreading, it would clearly make sense to at least try ramping up your outreach to this target group and see if the trend continued.

This isn't as crazy or unlikely as it sounds. I worked with one client on a campaign relating to pensions, and the client was convinced that fiftysomething conservative men would clearly be their sweet spot. They thought that, quite reasonably, these were the people most likely to have pension plans and to be most concerned with the solvency of those plans since they were so close to reaping the rewards from them.

It turned out, however, that the best responders and viralizers by far were twentysomething left-leaning women. As we discovered, there was a very potent gender-discrimination angle—that is, the specific type of pensions being protected were portable from job to job, as opposed to ones which required a full, uninterrupted career with one company. This might sound like an obscure, meaningless difference, but it's a big deal, since women are statistically more likely to have career interruptions to give birth to and raise young children. Thus, the audience most passionate about this effort, and most passionate about spreading the word about it, was an audience that wasn't even initially on the radar.

DIGGING INTO THE WEEDS AND tapping into the minds of multipliers isn't easy. It takes hard work and creativity, and a blend of art and science. But if you can figure out what makes the multipliers multiply and adjust your strategy accordingly, the rewards can make all this effort well worth it.

PART FIVE

JUMP-STARTING YOUR EFFORT

You've got your message, you've identified your messengers, and your campaign is moving.

But now you want to get things moving faster, and you've got some budget to make that happen.

This section will cover the best ways to do that—paid advertising and PR.

FIFTEEN

Advertising

The quickest way to jump-start your viral marketing effort is through paid advertising. This can be especially important at the beginning off your effort, when you're trying to reach a critical mass, such as enough people on a Facebook page to spur good conversation. You may be counting on viral spreading to drive your numbers over the long haul, but it's much easier to hit a viral tipping point if you have a good solid base to start from.

FOCUS ON RESULTS, FOCUS ONLINE

In general, the goal of advertising is to get a message out. You do so by paying people who already have large audiences to promote your message for you. That's basically what every TV, radio, newspaper, and online ad is. *Paying for the privilege of having multipliers multiply for you.* Sometimes the message is geared toward generating a specific outcome (clicks, sales, sign-ups), and sometimes it is more about generating awareness (getting people teed up for a more precise pitch that will come later). A movie ad, for example, weeks before the movie actually opens, is more about awareness. One running on a Friday evening when it's in the theaters is more about provoking a sale that night.

My advice to you would be to seek out advertising opportunities that are generated toward a specific, tangible, measurable outcome. Unless you are running millions of dollars of ads and can do before and after polling, it's really quite hard to measure the impact of an ad campaign on awareness. For those of us who don't have Fortune 500 budgets, focusing on a tangible, measurable outcome is the best way to judge the value of one ad versus another and to make adjustments to an ad strategy to maximize value.

Thus, in placing your ads, I'd strongly recommend focusing on ones that are directed toward clicks, sign-ups, sales, and other things that can actually be measured. I'd further recommend prioritizing advertising that gets you sign-ups—new fans, emails, and followers. Why pay to reach them just once when you can get them to sign up so you can keep reaching them again and again?

This also means focusing like a laser on the online medium. Yes, TV ads, radio ads, and newspaper ads are great and will impress your friends. But none of those mediums come even close to the cost effectiveness of online when it comes to generating sign-ups. When someone sees an ad online, they are one click away from being able to fan a Facebook page or sign up on a website. When they see one on TV or a newspaper, on the other hand, they probably will need to walk to their computer, maybe even turn it on, go to the site, and . . . well, by this time you've lost 95 percent of them. If you want to get the most out of your advertising dollar, focus online (aside from the caveat at the end of this chapter, where the buy is just a token buy to support an online effort).

I'll get to the places where you can place your ads in a minute, but first, let's get a little lay of the land and go over a few things you'll need to know, regardless of what venue you choose. The world of online advertising can sound scary to someone who's new to it, but don't worry, it's easier than it seems.

THE ELEMENTS THAT MAKE UP YOUR AD

First, there are the elements that make up the ad—image, text, or a combination of the two.

Image Ads

Image ads are most familiar as the banner ads you see on the top of many websites. They are what they sound like, just a simple image that when clicked takes the viewer to another site—the one that actually paid to stick the ad there. There is usually text in the ad, but it's actually part of the picture itself. The ads now sometimes show up on the sides of websites (primarily since people started instinctively ignoring the ads up top), and range in size, depending on the site.

To craft one of these image ads, you'll need to either hire a designer or use a design program yourself. Photoshop is probably the most popular program among designers, but can frankly be a little unnecessarily daunting for folks who are new to design. Most computers these days will include some kind of basic design program, which should be good for crafting a good, basic image for an ad. If you're willing to spend a little bit more (fifty-dollar range), I'm personally a big fan of Snagit (TechSmith.com), as mentioned earlier. It's a program that started out mainly for capturing screenshots (that is, "snag" it) but has evolved to include a very nice and intuitive design component (SnagIt Editor).

Note: You don't necessarily need to start from scratch when creating an image for an ad, but can use stock images or clip art. Sometimes, depending on the image requirements, this will be sufficient, but more often you'll use them as a part of what you're designing. As we discussed in Chapter 3, iStockphoto.com and

Microsoft clip art are good options for free or cheap images. Of course, the same caveat applies here as well—clip art does run the risk of looking generic, and if you have effective images of your own, consider using them instead.

When you create an image ad, make sure you understand the size and type requirements. Generally, places running the ads ("publishers") have pretty hard and fast rules, since they need to fit them into a set space on their sites. The "size" has two parts, typically: the actual width and height of the image (usually referred to in pixels) and the size of the file (how many bytes it is). Publishers like to keep the file size small, since the bigger it is, the longer it takes for the page to download. "Type" refers to the format of the image. The most common types on the web are JPEG and GIF, since all web browsers can "see" them, and since they generally create images that are smaller and quicker to download (as opposed to some other file formats, which are much higher resolution, and thus great for printing but a nightmare for downloading on a site).

If this sounds confusing, don't worry, it's actually easy. Pretty much every design program you use will have a "save as" option that allows you to save a file in any number of formats quite easily. Check the requirements of where you're advertising, but in general, JPEG or GIF should work pretty much anywhere online.

Text Ads

Text ads are ads that have just words and no image. The best known of these today are Google AdWords, which I'll discuss in Chapter 16. If you're not familiar with these, go to Google.com now, type "lawyer" in the search box, and note all the text ads that appear in the side column offering legal help. Next, try "dentist" and see how the ads change. Try several words, and take note of how the ads change instantly.

As with images, the precise requirements of the text ad will vary, depending on where you're placing them. In general, however, the rules for crafting an optimal text ad are similar to crafting a compelling Facebook or Twitter post or press release headline (see Chapter 20). Keep it short, simple, and compelling—and focused on the audience viewing it and the desired action. If you want them to click over to a site, for example, craft the text so it leaves them hanging and gives them a reason to click (say, a question where the answer requires a click). And don't forget the other lessons you've already learned regarding compelling content (humor, sex appeal, "problem" causing, etc.).

For example:

- **Are you single? Love wine? Click to check out our new "wine lovers" matchmaking service!**

- **Poetry with "balls"? You bet! Read some right now!**

- **Which team's baseball caps outsell even the Yankees? Click to find out!**

The specific shape and size will depend on the ad venue, of course, but the bottom line is that you're not looking to tell the full story—you're looking for them to click over to get to the full story.

Combination Image and Text Ads

Finally, there are combination ads. On the web, these are probably most common in blogs (especially ones that use BlogAds .com, which I'll discuss in Chapter 17). Go to PerezHilton.com, for example, and look in the side column, where you'll notice a slew of ads that have images and text just below them. These are also the standard format for Facebook ads (see Chapter 18).

In this case, you'll need to provide an image and some accompanying text. Typically, the image is the "grabber," the thing that catches the eye, and the text offers a bit more explanation to entice the click. So focus on getting the right image first and then crafting the accompanying text (this is counterintuitive, but the image really is more important). For example, let's say you're selling a book about food recipes for toddlers. Your instinct might be to just use a picture of the book cover, since that's what's being sold, along with some text giving the book's title and a short description. Perhaps, but you'll probably get more attention and clicks with a close-up of a screaming toddler's face and text starting off with, "Is mealtime hell? Learn recipes your toddler will love . . ."

THERE ARE OTHER AD FORMATS, of course, that get more elaborate, offering animation, video, and other options. However, for most folks, image, text, or image-text combination is what you'll use, and most certainly where you should start.

WHAT DO YOU WANT TO PAY FOR? TIME, CLICKS, OR VIEWS?

When placing an ad online, there are typically three ways you can pay: by time duration of ad, by views, or by clicks.

Time Duration

Duration of ad is the oldest option, and usually the most straightforward, at least on the surface. You agree on a time duration—day, week, month, whatever—and your ad runs for that time period. If you go this option, however, make sure to find out how many times your ad will actually be seen. Most reliable options should be able to give you a good estimate, based on past performance. Make sure that "past performance" is based on a long enough history, however, to be a true indicator. If you're buying an ad for a week, for example, get weekly traffic on the site for the last few months. If you see lots of wild swings up and down, just be aware that you're risking that your ad might show up in one of the "down" weeks.

You'll also want to know in this case where exactly your ad will appear on these sites. The higher on the page, the better. A term often used is "above the fold," meaning that someone will see your ad when they first come to the site and not have to scroll down. This is important, since most people aren't going to scroll down on a typical site. Thus, the ad below the fold might be up as long, but be actually *seen* a fraction of the time. It doesn't mean you should rule out below the fold, if the price is right, but do be aware that the difference in performance will be significant.

By View (CPM)

Pay per view is another option, one that generally gained popularity because so many folks wanted to know in the early days how many views a day/week/month actually meant. It's also a nice way for sites with enormous amounts of page views to break up their ad buys in more manageable, bite-size chunks for clients.

Typically, you'll hear the term "CPM" used to describe this, meaning "cost per thousand views" (with the Roman numeral *M* used for thousand). If someone tells you "Our CPM is $10," it means that you will pay $10 every thousand times your ad is viewed.

As with time-duration ads, it makes a big difference whether you're above or below the fold.

By Click (CPC)

Finally, there is cost per click, or CPC. This was initially popularized by Google, but has gained widespread popularity among other publishers as well. In this case, you pay each time someone clicks on your ad. If the CPC is 50 cents, it means you pay 50 cents whenever someone clicks it.

Typically, you set some kind of maximum budget, after which your ad no longer appears.

By the way, a common fear is that some jerk (competitor, opponent, or just plain jerk) will see your ad and just keep clicking it over and over again until your budget is depleted. Most of the serious publishers (Google and Facebook, for example), however, have safeguards to prevent this.

CPC has another interesting twist to it, when it comes to developing your strategy. With CPM and time duration, you want your ad to be clicked as many times as humanly possible—and you should strive to make your ads as compelling and click-worthy as you can. With CPC, however, since you're paying for clicks, you actually don't want it to be *too* compelling. More accurately, you want it to be compelling, but only to your target audience. You don't want a lot of curiosity clickers who will cost you money but never actually become a fan of your page, sign up on your website, or buy your product.

Let's say you were selling dog food, for example. If you were going the time-duration or CPM route, you might want to use a picture of the world's cutest puppy as an attention grabber. Everyone loves puppies, right? With a CPC route, however, you would not want to do that. The last thing you want is to be flooded with clicks from people who don't actually own dogs, but just are smitten by this adorable pooch. You might want to use a less charismatic dog, or something else that appeals only to dog owners (say, a poop scoop).

In the CPC case, you also might actually prefer to be *below* the fold. Again, since you're paying for clicks, you're looking for clickers who are the most serious about what you have to sell to them. Someone who pokes around on a site a bit and scrolls down to look for more may well be more serious than someone just passing through.

PICKING PLACES TO ADVERTISE

It's a big, big web, and just about all the sites out there would love to have your advertising dollars. I'll go into a few of my favorite venues in a minute—Google, BlogAds.com, and Facebook—but since the choices are nearly infinite, here are some things to keep in mind as you start your foray into advertising:

Test, Test, Test
I can't stress this enough. Don't put all your eggs in one basket, and don't put all your advertising dollars into one publisher. Buy your ads in bite-size chunks, at least to start, and then buy more

of the ones that actually produce results. Typically, most advertising venues will give you click-through stats that show you which ads were most compelling. That's a good start, but if your goal lies beyond the click—say, sign-ups or sales—then you'll want to track effectiveness on your own website as well.

The way you track this will depend on which platform you use to host your site. Most of them, however, will allow you to use a small tracking suffix with the ads. As with the approach discussed earlier for tracking email effectiveness (see Chapter 12), this involves adding a small suffix (such as "?ad1" or "?ad2") to the end of the URL to which the ads point. Thus, MariosWine Shop.com in two different ads would become the following:

- **http://MariosWineShop.com?ad1**

- **http://MariosWineShop.com?ad2**

Both would send the clicker to the exact same site, but that site's analytics tool would be able to differentiate which visits came from which ads, and (ideally) which sign-ups or sales came from them as well. That's pretty important. It might be great to know that both your ads were getting a phenomenal click-through rate, but if one were resulting in ten times the sales or sign-ups as the other, that piece of data would be far more relevant.

Get Data from the Publisher

Find out what their target audience is, how many views you can expect, where you'll be on the page, and anything else you can. You'll need this to make an informed judgment when comparing publisher options.

Be Wary of Big Name Brands

In my experience, some of the best-known publishers are frankly the biggest rip-offs. This is especially the case for publishers that are primarily known for an offline property—TV network, newspaper, or magazine. Time and time again I have seen marquee name sites charging ten, fifty, or even one hundred (!!!) times as much for CPM rates as a lesser-known site or blog that is attracting essentially the same audience.

Look for Flexibility

Some publishers, such as Facebook, BlogAds.com, and Google, allow you to change ads, while others require you to submit an ad and stick with it. This is typically the case for publishers that place the ads themselves, as opposed to letting you do it via an interface. On the one hand, it's not a big deal to have to commit to a week or even more, and it's understandable why some of these venues don't want to deal with constantly changing an ad. On the other hand, it's nice to have the flexibility to shift an ad if something breaks in the news, for example, and you want to ride that wave. It's even nicer if you want to have the option of trying a few versions and seeing what works best.

THE ONE "ONLINE ONLY" CAVEAT: USING TV, RADIO, OR MAGAZINE ADS AS VIRAL HOOKS

There is one caveat to the "focus online" rule. If you are creating a non-online ad that is primarily acting as a viral hook for your online effort, then it might make sense.

For example, back in 2003, I started an effort called Draft WesleyClark.com that was focused on drafting General Wesley Clark to enter the race for president. It was a very shoestring, barebones effort, with almost no budget, a strong online focus, and a specific focus on getting supporters to visit the site to write letters to General Clark, asking him to run.

Trying to run a real TV ad campaign would have frankly been asinine. Short of spending millions, there was no way that a TV ad campaign could've been big enough to generate tens of thousands or even thousands of letters. And "millions" was "millions more" than we had in the bank.

Enter Bud Jackson, a veteran political TV ad producer with hundreds of campaigns to his credit and enough trophies to fill a U-Haul. Bud was a fan of General Clark and gave me a call, offering to help. After a lot of brainstorming with Bud and one of the other leaders of the effort, Josh Margulies, we managed to come up with a plan that made sense:

- **Produce a solid TV ad as cheaply as possible (in this case, the budget was under $1,800).**

- **Pony up another few thousand to run it on TV, with almost all of the buys being on small cable channels and overnight (where and when the price was far cheaper).**

- **Put out a press release to reporters and an email to our supporters, announcing the new ad that would run "hundreds of times" on TV—and directing them to the DraftWesleyClark.com site to view it.**

Now, we didn't tell people that each of the "hundreds of times" was costing about five to ten dollars (really, these were tiny stations and late at night). We didn't lie, we just didn't tell them.

The net result? This was viewed as a big, big deal. It was the first presidential TV ad of the 2004 campaign, and it was being done by a grassroots group. There was an enormous wave of media coverage, with the ad appearing on a slew of national news programs, sometimes run in its entirety (something we could have never paid for!). And there was an even bigger wave of supporter enthusiasm and viralization. This was pre-YouTube, when viewing and spreading a video online was rather painful. And yet, it still spread like wildfire, generating thousands of sign-ups for the effort and hundreds of thousands of views of the website.

It was easily one of the most successful efforts I've led, in terms of bang for the buck. But again, it worked because the TV ad was seen due to news coverage viralization, not because we paid a zillion dollars to buy these views.

This is a tactic I've used a number of times. During the Just SayBlow.com campaign (the one tweaking George W. Bush for his antidrug stance, while refusing to discuss his own past cocaine use), we produced a radio ad with a humorous, edgy spin (the listener could hear fake sniffing in the background, as if cocaine were being snorted).

The real hook in that case, however, was the choice of where to run the ad. We announced, tongue-in-cheek, that we had picked three "strategically significant" cities: Coke, Texas; Powderhorn, Colorado; and Blowville, Ohio (yes, they all exist). We put this out to reporters, in a press release, and to supporters via email. Everyone snickered at the snarky coke references, and again, we got some wonderful coverage and viralization (even though it was the "ancient" web days of 2001).

In that example, we also spent very little on the actual paid buy (a few hundred dollars). But the right viral combination (humor, villain, and timeliness) worked to spread it in spite of that.

In both these cases (and several others I love, but will spare you the details of) the return on investment was off the charts, and producing ads for TV and radio was a critical part of that. It gave credibility, and it was frankly interesting content. But again, remember, the paid ad buy was quite small, and the goal was ultimately to produce buzz and viral spreading that was earned, and not bought.

IF YOU'RE LOOKING TO JUMP-START a marketing effort, there's really no better tool than paid advertising. And with the options we're about to explore in the next few chapters, it's possible for even the little guy to get that jump-start without breaking the bank.

SIXTEEN

Using Google AdWords

Google AdWords (Google.com/AdWords) is a place where many new advertisers choose to start. With Google AdWords, you pay for the right to have your text ad appear in a sidebar when someone searches for a designated term. In the "lawyer" example from earlier, the ads you see in the sidebar are for people who paid to show up along that term. The more they paid, the higher their ads appear in the column. While Google offers a few options, my recommendation is to start with text only, and with CPC pricing.

Google ads can be a good place to start for folks new to advertising, since they can be text-only (that is, just a keyboard and a few minutes is all it takes), and the interface is reasonably non-threatening. Further, it's easy to place many ads at once but still have a low overall budget, something that makes it a particularly good venue for those just learning how to test ad effectiveness.

Google ads are particularly good for products or services that people are likely to search for on Google, and for which there are logical search keywords that demonstrate a potential interest in that item. For example, if you were a band, promoting your new album, or an author promoting your new book, it would be pretty logical to buy an ad tied to your name. Someone searching for it would be highly likely to be a fan, or at least someone with an interest in learning more. If you were an orthodontist setting up a practice in Des Moines, the odds are pretty good that someone searching for "Des Moines orthodontist" would be a hot prospect.

But let's say you were running a petition effort targeting a very polarizing public figure, say, Sarah Palin or Michael Moore. The challenge in that case is that half the searches might be people who like the figure and half might be people who dislike the figure. Either way, you'd end up with a low click-through rate, or a lot of clicks from people whose opinions were exactly opposite what you were seeking.

Bottom line, Google tells you what people are searching for, but it doesn't tell you why.

GETTING STARTED

If you do decide to proceed with an ad on Google, the process is fairly straightforward and reasonably user-friendly. Once you set up an account and are ready to place your ad, Google will lead you through the steps to create your ad.

First, you'll be prompted to write it. You don't have a ton of leeway here, just twenty-five characters for the headline, two lines of text to follow, and a link to what you're advertising.

Next, you'll be asked who you'd like to target. In this step, you can choose things like location and language. Make sure to choose carefully, based on your goals and target audience. You'll also choose whether to have your ads appear just on Google itself, or on Google partner sites (other search sites and sites that display ads based on the content on their own pages). This frankly matters less in my opinion, though again, you may want to try both ways, and see if you have different results with the different ads.

Finally, you'll choose the keywords you want to appear next to and the price you're willing to pay to do so. Because Google actually gives you precise performance data for each separate keyword, my recommendation is to choose a whole slew of keywords—at least a few dozen. If you're advertising a wine shop, for example, use Merlot, Cabernet, Port, Madeira, Shiraz, and other varieties. If you're advertising a poetry book, try poetry, verse, and maybe a few names of poets whose work is similar to your own. Google will suggest keywords for you as well.

In terms of bidding for each word, Google will also suggest a price for each, based on how popular a keyword is. If the price is far higher than would make sense for you, and simply not worth it, don't bother. For example, it seems like every lawyer on the planet is already advertising for the keyword "lawyer," so you wouldn't have a heck of a lot of luck showing up in that sidebar unless you were willing to a spend a whole lot. But if Google's suggested price is close enough to be reasonable, my advice would be to bid on the low end, and then slowly reduce your bid over time, as long as you are still getting clicks.

For example, let's say you're placing an ad for your wine shop, and Google suggests a bid of "68 cents to 89 cents" for the keyword "Cabernet." Okay, first, if you're thinking that you'll just try a bid of 1 cent, think again. Google's a zillion-dollar company, and they're smarter than that. Even 5 or 10 cents will probably be a waste of time. At best, you might pop up a few times, way, way down below the other ads, never to be clicked. Instead, try starting with something more reasonable, say, 40 or 50 cents per click. If that doesn't work, bump it up to the bottom of Google's range, 68 cents. That sometimes seems to get things going. Once you start getting some clicks, you can try slowly reducing the price and see how low you can go while still getting them.

That should get you started, and you should typically see

results within a few hours (there is an approval process, but Google is pretty quick about it).

CRAFTING YOUR AD

Assuming you've chosen the CPC option, as recommended above, remember that your goal is to write an ad that is good— but not *too* good. Your goal is not to get as many clicks as possible, it's to get as many clicks as possible from your specific target audience.

Don't set the bar too high, however. If your ad ends up getting an extremely low click-through rate, Google will automatically bump up the CPC price required for it to continue showing. Your best bet is to go with something that is interesting and has a hook, but also makes clear what it is that you actually want the clicker to do, once he or she has clicked.

If you're adverting your wine tasting, for example, you might want to go with something like the following:

Wine Tasting: 5/25
Try the wonderful wines of Italy
without even leaving Fargo
MariosWineShop.com

Simple, straightforward, to the point. A clicker knows exactly what's in store and, unless he or she is interested, at least fleetingly, is unlikely to click.

If you were selling a poetry book, one with an edgier focus, you might want to try something like the following:

Poetry with Balls
Who says poetry has to be boring?
Buy "Extreme Poetry." Just $9.95
ExtremePoetry.com

This one is a little more playful, and you might get a few more curiosity seekers. Then again, the clear "buy" ask should hopefully frighten off those with no intention whatsoever of plunking down $9.95. Of course, this is where testing comes in.

Repeating and Optimizing

Once you've placed your first ad, consider placing a bunch more (Google makes it easy to clone and tweak them), with different headlines and text. Then track the performance of all your ads like a hawk, pause the ones that are not doing well, and take the ones that are doing well, see what's working, and try to come up with new ads that do it even better.

IF YOU'RE JUST GETTING STARTED in the world of advertising, Google AdWords can be a good place to do it. It's simple, it's well established, and even if you don't end up using it for the long haul, the odds are that it will be a nice gateway to what you do end up using.

S E V E N T E E N

Advertising on Blogs

I'm a big fan of advertising on blogs. They attract a segment of the Internet population that is highly engaged, passionate about a specific subject, and willing (and eager) to talk about that subject with great conviction (whether it's informed or not varies by the person, of course). Engaged, passionate, and eager to talk—just the kind of people you want to reach to spur viral spreading. You may want to start your first foray into advertising on Google, but once you're ready to ramp things up a bit, blogs are well worth a shot.

If you're looking to advertise on blogs, I'd strongly recommend checking out BlogAds.com. It's by far my favorite way to advertise on blogs. BlogAds.com is essentially a middleman between the advertisers and the publishers (the blogs). Several thousand blogs have made a partnership with the company, whereby BlogAds.com can sell ads on their behalf.

This means that you as an advertiser can go to the site, choose from thousands of blogs, place your ads on any number of them that you wish, and complete the transaction in one fell swoop. This is far, far easier than going to the blogs one by one, given that almost all of them are one-man/woman shops.

CHOOSING YOUR BLOGS

To start the process, go to BlogAds.com and click on the "Advertisers" link. At this point, you'll have a choice of going to the full list of blogs, or going to "hives," subgroups of blogs categorized by subject area (everything from "television" to "love" to "conservative"). The hives approach is nice if you find one that really matches with your goals. If you were selling gourmet food, for example, there's actually a "Foodblog" hive with nearly a hundred blogs. Alternatively, you can go to the full list and then search by category—keywords, political affiliation, city, and a host of other items. If you go the hives route, I'd still recommend checking out the full list, since not every blog is a member of the relevant hive (without getting into the gory details, the hives are self-organized and not everyone joins).

Once you've decided which blogs might be of interest, you'll want to narrow it down based on two items: estimated CPM and number of ads already on the blog. BlogAds.com lists the CPM (reminder, the price per thousand views) in a column in the full list, making it very easy to spot the potential bargains. There is a huge range here, with some blogs priced at CPM's of $10 or higher, and others priced at 10 *cents*. That's a hundredfold difference!

Before you jump at the bargains, however, check and look how many ads are already running on the blog. I've seen some with twenty or higher at one time. With that much competition, you're not going to get a whole lot of click-throughs, or even eyeballs. Typically, though, most blogs will have between zero and five running at any given time. Try to weigh the two together as you prioritize your blog choices—a CPM of 10 cents is great, but if it has five ads already, and another blog with a CPM of 20 cents has zero, the latter will almost certainly be a better choice.

Now that you've narrowed it down, and you're closer to the "buy" step, make sure to visit the blogs. The descriptions on BlogAds.com are generally good but written by the bloggers themselves, so you'll want to see them yourself to make sure they're appropriate. Look to see if the tone and content feels right for your target audience. Note: Most of these blogs are not quite G-rated, and some are frankly X-rated. You'll want to make sure you're comfortable with your ad being associated with the blogs you choose.

At this point, you can pick which blogs you want and how long you want your ad to run—a week, two weeks, a month, or three months. Some blogs offer deep discounts for longer periods, so take this into account. However, you might see radically different performance on different blogs, so you might want to test for a week before going for a quarter-year commitment!

CRAFTING YOUR AD

Next, you create your ad, a combination of a headline, an image, and text. Now, remember, with blog ads you are paying for the time duration of your ad rather than per click. Your goal should be to get as many clicks as humanly possible.

For the headline and image, follow the advice from Chapter 15. The image is designed to grab an eyeball and get attention, and the headline is your quick hook, to get them to read more.

For the text, however, you can get a little more elaborate. Try to use as much of the three hundred characters as possible, including inserting spaces, since the longer your ad is, the more space it will take up on the blog. That is, it's not a set area, it stretches if there is more text. Also, you can include hyperlinks in the text itself, which I'd recommend doing. By default, the image is linked to your page, as is a "read more" blurb that is automatically inserted at the end of the text. Still though, having links within the text gives the viewer more chance to click, so go ahead and make it easy for them.

This also is your chance to include links to a few places. With ActForLove.org, for example, the dating site mentioned earlier, I found it effective to include links to "men seeking women," "women seeking men," "men seeking men," and "women seeking women." They all linked back to the same site, but appeared to make the clicking just a little more compelling, since it put the viewer one click away from their specific interest.

Here's one of the ad versions I used that did particularly well:

HEADLINE: Good Soul, Good Karma, GREAT ASS!

IMAGE: Face of attractive man or woman (rotated)

BODY COPY:

ActForLove.org: The dating site for Democratic, liberal, and progressive activists. (As seen in NY Times)

—>Women Seeking Men

—>Men Seeking Women

—>Men Seeking Men

—>Women Seeking Women

ActForLove.org: Because a hot bod should have a good heart too.

The image was the eye-catcher. An attractive person, but not absurdly or sleazily so. Someone the audience would see as a real person, not a supermodel, but still find attractive.

The headline was the eyebrow raiser. The "good soul, good karma" part established that this was aimed at a lefty audience, but the "GREAT ASS" part made it stand out (and yes, I'm sure it offended some people—humorless sorts we wouldn't want anyway). But it was also deliberately used as a filter. ActForLove.org might have been aimed at lefty activists, but ones with a sense of humor and fun, not the whiner contingent.

The text itself was straightforward, to explain what ActForLove.org was, but also wedged in a *New York Times* reference to establish credibility.

The performance of this ad, in terms of click-throughs and sign-ups, was just off the charts.

Another version simply changed the title to "Tired of dating Republicans?" and the image to an arguing (but still attractive) couple. A completely different angle and hook, but same text, and same stellar performance.

For another ad, I went with a much simpler approach:

HEADLINE: Democratic Dates!

IMAGE: Face of attractive woman, very close up, looking right into the camera

BODY COPY: ActForLove.org: Dates for Democrats. Because a great bod should have a great heart and mind to match.

Again, stellar performance.

The ads that *didn't* perform well? The ones that tried to make a more cerebral pitch, based on the "activism" component, rather than the sex appeal lure. (See Chapter 11 and note that even ardent lefty activists are still just well-dressed monkeys at heart).

OPTIMIZING YOUR ADS

Once you've created your ad, it's time to play with a few different versions to see what works best, as per my ActForLove.org example.

BlogAds.com gives you the option of creating a few different versions of ads for the same buy and weighing how often they are shown (50/50 percent, 90/10 percent, whatever/whatever). These different versions will be automatically rotated (not shown concurrently). Never pass up an opportunity to test. Give it a shot, using at least one other version.

Specifically, I would recommend trying a few different images. This really is the main thing that catches eyeballs, so try a few different ones, even if you keep the rest of the ad identical. If you test nothing else, test that. If you go further, try different headlines. And ideally, go even further, and try different approaches altogether.

Once your ads are running, BlogAds.com gives good, updated data on click-through rates. In this case, the higher the click-through, the better (again with the caveat that if you are striving for sales or sign-ups or something else you can measure, that takes even higher priority). If you have a few versions of an ad rotating on the blog, and one is performing significantly better, then change that one to run 100 percent of the time. Even with that top-performing one, however, make sure to change the image every few days, so repeat visitors are jolted to pay attention again.

Becoming Part of the Conversation

Beyond that, there's one trick in particular that I love doing with blog ads—shifting ads based on the conversation within the blog itself. It's a wonderful little trick, and one that I am shocked is not used more often since it dramatically increases the chances of spurring conversation within the blog itself, and thus giving you the added benefit of an echo beyond your ad.

For example, let's say you're advertising your wine shop on a food blog. Let's say the blogger posts a story about Brie cheese. Why not shift your ad to something like "Love Brie? We have wonderful wines to go with that." Or if you're hawking baseball caps, and the blogger writes a post about the Chicago Cubs, change it to something like "The Cubbies could finally win the World Series this year—wouldn't you love to be wearing a Cubs hat when it happens?" BlogAds.com allows you to make these changes almost instantly (no reapproval required), so you can use this trick again and again and again.

From my experience, most bloggers and visitors to the blog find it amusing or even flattering that the advertisers are actually paying attention. Some, of course, find it a little creepy, and will say so. But who cares? As long as they're making comments for any reason, they're almost certainly going to generate more clicks for you. And in a world where "one in one thousand" is considered a good click-through rate, "a few more clicks" could mean the difference between a subpar ad and a blockbuster.

WHEN IT COMES TO REACHING an engaged audience that has opinions and likes to share those opinions, advertising on blogs is a fantastic option. If you take the time to seek out the right blogs, and you go the extra mile to get creative with your advertising, you might find that this is the perfect audience to tap into for clicks, evangelism, and a whole lot of multiplying.

EIGHTEEN

Facebook Advertising

t's hard to overestimate the value of Facebook on the advertising front. This holds true whether you're using the ads to lure people to a page on Facebook itself or an external website.

Because Facebook has such a large audience, and because that audience supplies so much information about themselves (gender, age, interests, school, work, etc.), it's possible to target people with unbelievable precision and still reach a critical mass.

Think of it this way—if I asked you what country drinks the most beer, what would you say? Germany? England? The United States? Actually, it's China. Simply by virtue of its size, it drinks the most, even though those other countries might drink much more per person. The same holds true for Facebook. With more than half a billion members, nearly any category of individuals can be found en masse there, and in greater numbers than even communities targeted solely toward that specific category.

Don't believe me? Consider the following:

- **You want female fans of the Beatles, between eighteen and thirty, and in Wisconsin? Facebook has 91,260 of them.**

- **You want fans of Captain Crunch who are fifty or older? There are over six hundred.**

- **Want men who like men *and* wine, but only in Utah? There are over one hundred.**

If you know who your target audience is, the odds are you're going to find them on Facebook. And given that your advertising is being done in a highly viral environment, a supporter gained via Facebook is much more valuable to you than a supporter gained via the web. It's better to get someone that you know hangs out in a viral environment, and is thus more likely to be a multiplier, than a random person you only hope does.

Further, unlike Google, Facebook keywords usually indicate an affinity. Someone searching on Google for "Sarah Palin" might love her or might hate her. But someone with Sarah Palin as a "like" in their Facebook profile almost certainly has an affinity for her.

SETTING YOUR STRATEGY

Here's what you'll need to consider before starting a Facebook advertising campaign.

Goal
What will define whether an ad is successful? Are you looking for sign-ups? Sales? Something else? Make sure to get specific. An ad that's getting clicks like gangbusters might be great, but if your goal is sales and those clicks aren't converting to them, the ad isn't really a success.

Budget

How much do you want to spend? Over what period of time? The good news about Facebook is that there is no minimum buy. The better news is that even a relative novice can create a decent ad without the help of a designer. Thus, it's possible to spend even less than a hundred dollars and still get results. The more you spend, of course, the greater your results will be. So be frugal, but if your goals are big, be realistic about the budget you'll need. As a rule of thumb, assume that you'll pay about a dollar per click and see how that synchs up with your goals to guesstimate how many clicks and how much budget you'll need. (Note: You can also choose a CPM approach for your ad, and guesstimate a budget on that basis, but in general, my recommendation is to go the CPC route.)

Target Audience

Who do you want to reach? Refer back to the target audience bio you put together in Chapter 2. Get as precise as possible regarding demographics. Are you targeting just men? Women? Seniors? People only in a certain city or region? What types of interests would your ideal targets likely have in their profiles? If you're advertising a new wine shop, for example, people with "wine" or "Merlot" or "Cabernet" in their profiles would be eminently logical potential customers. If you're opening a pizza shop, then finding people who like "pizza" would be a natural.

The more precisely you can define your target audience and your goals, the more effective your campaign will be.

PLACING YOUR ADS

Once you've got your goals and targets in mind, you're ready to place the ads. If you're already logged in to Facebook, look for the link to "Advertising" and click on it. Next, click "Create an Ad."

Facebook's instructions for the basic mechanics of this are pretty good, but we'll go through these one by one.

Enter the Thing You Want to Advertise

This may be a page you have on Facebook, or it might be a website. You should either select the Facebook page from the drop-down list or enter the URL of the website.

Pick a Headline (Title) for the Ad

If you click on "I have something I want to advertise on Facebook," you'll be forced to use the exact name of the page. That's not a bad thing, and it comes with the advantage that people can become fans of your page by clicking "like" on the ad itself. But if you don't want to use the title, then click on the option for advertising something "not on Facebook," and enter the full URL of the Facebook page. The ad will still point to your Facebook page, but you'll have the flexibility to use another title. Note: Regardless of which path you choose, you'll be restricted to twenty-five characters here, so be tight with your wording.

The rules for a good headline for a Facebook ad are directionally similar to those for a Google ad (see Chapter 16). Assuming you're going the CPC route, you're trying to come up with a good hook that works for your target audience, not curiosity clickers who will never buy what it is you have to sell. So, again, if you're promoting a wine tasting, consider something like "Wine Tasting: 5/25." If you're promoting an edgy poetry book, something like "Poetry with Balls" could do the trick. The caveat here, however, is that if you've really honed in on your target audience well, you should have a lot less of a problem with the "never interested, only curious" types. This can afford you a bit more creativity on the headline, and indeed the ad as a whole.

Enter Text in the Body

You'll be restricted to 135 characters here, so you've got a bit more leeway, but not a ton. Try to come up with something provocative that makes the viewer curious and provokes a click. Asking a question can be effective, for example, if the viewer needs to click on the ad in order to get the answer.

Again, be careful. If you're paying per click, you'll want to make sure that people who click are actually your target audience and not random curious people who would never be interested in what you're selling. If you're advertising your new wine shop, for example, it might make sense to have a question such as "Which wine is more popular in America, Merlot or Cabernet?" It wouldn't make sense, on the other hand to have a completely unrelated question, such as "Which performer has sold more albums, Eminem or Lady Gaga?" That's an extreme example, of course, but the bottom line is that you want to always make sure you're targeting your actual targets.

If you're advertising a page on Facebook, and your goal is to get people to become fans of it (to "like" the page), I'd strongly recommend being quite overt about it. For an ad for Left Action, for example, the page geared toward lefty activists, I used the following text:

- **Click "like" if you're stunned Sarah Palin is STILL being taken seriously as a potential PRESIDENT. Then let's work to prevent it!**

The response was enormous. In one click, people could express a preference regarding Sarah Palin, and concurrently "like" the organization that brought them that ad.

Promoting your new bakery? Consider something along the following lines:

- **Click "like" if you want the chance to win a free, gooey, yummy, chocolatey cupcake from Valley Stream's newest family bakery.**

That ad would work particularly well if you were targeting people who are fans of cupcakes (nearly two hundred thousand of them on Facebook, by the way, and more joining every day).

Pick an Image

You won't have a lot of leeway here, since the image is only 110 pixels wide by 80 tall. Basically, you'll want something that would look good on a postage stamp. So think close-up and with one strong focus. This isn't the place for a crowd shot of thousands. Just like the icon you pick for your page, you'll want to get something that is eye-catching and really stands out.

Also, think in terms of what will appeal to your target audience. Wine shop? Great, what about a nice bottle of wine? Pizza shop? How about a yummy-looking slice? If your ad is going to run for more than a few days, be prepared to switch images, since once your target audience sees the first one a few times, the odds are slim that they'll click the next time they see it.

Choose Your Targeting

Next, set the rules for who exactly will see your ad. Those who do not match your criteria will not see it.

Some of the categories are pretty obvious—gender, age, location, relationship status, education, and workplace. If you have determined that your target audience falls into specific groups within those categories, go ahead and set them.

Once you have those set, you're ready to choose interests. These are things that the Facebook users have self-identified as their interests, either by putting them in their profiles or liking a page of that name. This is where you can enter anything from "the Beatles" to "pizza" to "surfing" to . . . pretty much anything. Get creative, play around, and try a bunch of terms.

Note, however, that when you add more terms, it gives you the number of people who are interested in *at least* one (as opposed to all of them). So if you enter "pizza" and "the Beatles" it will show you people who are interested in at least one, though not necessarily both. If you are targeting interests like this that are wildly different, you'd be best off doing two separate ads. On the other hand, if you were targeting cake lovers for your bakery ad, it would be fine to include in the same ad logically related keywords, such as cake, cupcake, and pie.

Next, decide if you want to advertise based on "Connections on Facebook." This allows you to target people who are connected to pages that you run on Facebook. And I mean "you" literally. The person placing the ads must also be the admin of the pages targeted for them to show up as options. If you are having someone else place the ads, this is easily solvable by just making them an admin as well. But make sure you trust them, because once they're an admin, they'll also be able to post messages on the page (to all fans) and do anything else that an admin can do, for good or ill.

At this point, you will want to determine if you have a critical mass. On the page where you're crafting the ad, you should see a number for "estimated reach." This figure shows the total number of people who fit the variables you've indicated and who could see the ad. You'll notice as you change variables, the number updates automatically. Generally, you'll want this number to be at least in the thousands or higher when you place the ad. Once you start getting below that, you're unlikely to get more than a few dozen clicks, if that, given that even the best click-through rate rarely exceeds 1 percent. So target, and target precisely, but try not to get too small an audience. On the flip side, if you see a number in the millions, you may be casting too wide a net. Consider narrowing your scope if you want to maximize ad performance and return on your investment.

Set Your Budget and Time Frame

Finally, it's time to indicate how long you want the ads to run and what you're willing to pay.

- **BUDGET: Set the maximum amount you'll want to pay per day. Facebook may actually restrict you to a lower amount, until you've made a few payments, and they've determined you're good for the money (the limit maxes out at $5,000 per day, but Facebook will raise it on a case-by-case basis).**

- **SCHEDULE: If there's a specific time frame to your campaign (say, you're advertising an event happening in three days), go** ahead and set it. If not, you can just leave it open, and the ad will keep running. If you're the forgetful type, however, you might want to set it for a week or two, to ensure you don't accidentally end up racking up charges.

- CPM VERSUS CPC: Typically, I recommend that people pay per each click since that's generally the goal—getting someone to actually click over to see and interact with what it is you're advertising. However, if it's a case where you really are just trying to promote awareness of something (for example, reminding people that it's Election Day), then you might want to consider CPM (cost per thousand views). Why? Because even if people don't click, they may still see the ad and have at least a slight increase in awareness.

- MAKE YOUR BID: This is the point where you tell Facebook what you're willing to pay per click or thousand views. Facebook will suggest a range, but you can put in anything you want. Of course, if you put in "one cent per click," then the odds are almost certain that someone else will outbid you for those targets, and their ad will appear instead of yours. I've found that the best bet is to set it at the low end of the range that Facebook recommends, and then slowly lower it, as long as you're still getting results.

Once you've set up your ad, you'll need to wait for Facebook to actually approve the ad before it starts running. Sometimes this can happen within minutes. Sometimes, it can take hours (especially if the ad is placed outside of typical U.S. business hours).

Repeat and Optimize
You've placed your first ad, and that's just wonderful. Now it's time to place more.

The odds are slim that you're going to hit a grand slam with your first ad. Fortunately, because Facebook does not require a minimum spend per ad, you can try running several concurrently, watch their respective performance, and then simply "pause" the ads that are not working as effectively. Try coming up with at least five your first time, just for comparison.

Try testing the same ad with different demographic targets. You may be surprised what a difference you can find based on something you might not think would be important. I routinely find a fairly large gap in the response rates of males and females to the same ad, even for campaigns where the ad or thing being advertised doesn't appear to have any logical gender bias. In other cases, I've seen a fairly large gap based on age. Interestingly enough, neither of these gaps appears to be consistent, instead flipping back and forth depending on the ad.

You should also try testing duplicate ads targeting different keywords. Going back to the example of your new wine shop, you might think it's eminently logical to target fans of wine and Cabernet and Merlot. An ad targeting all three keywords would make sense. But if you did three ads, each targeting one of the keywords, you could see which one performed the best. It might be that someone who specified "Merlot" or "Cabernet" as opposed to just "wine" was a more serious wine drinker, more likely to go to a wine shop rather than a supermarket, and thus, more likely to click on your ad. Alternatively, it might be the case that the "wine" people were more willing to try a range of wines, and in fact would welcome a specialty store with more unusual and higher end choices. Which theory is right? Try both, and find out.

If creating multiple ads sounds like a pain, well, it is, a little. But Facebook offers an option to create a duplicate ad with one click, while you're editing it. You'll need to go in and manually change the keywords or demographic targeting, or whatever else is different. But the image and content will be there, no recreating necessary.

ADVERTISING TO YOUR OWN PAGES

Here's a common mistake that way, way too many Facebook aficionados make when it comes to marketing. They don't put up ads targeting their own page members. Why? Because they assume, "Hell, if I can send them updates, why would I need to advertise to them?"

Well, here's why—a status update will typically only be seen by a few percent, at most, of your fan base. Most simply aren't logged on at the right time or don't see the posts because Facebook's weird and spooky algorithm hasn't surfaced it for them.

Nevertheless, those people clearly are still very much interested in what you have to say, right? That's why they signed up in the first place. So go ahead and show them ads! Think of it this way—if you were a musician with a fan page on Facebook, it would certainly be worth it to advertise to your fans that you were releasing a new album, right? And if you were an author, with a new book coming out, this would be a logical audience to hit, right? The same holds true for nearly any product. Frankly, it's arguable that the prime benefit of getting fans for a page is not in fact to be able to reach them via updates—but to identify them clearly as your key target audience for further pitches.

ADVERTISING TO PAGES WITH HIGH CONCENTRATIONS OF YOUR FANS

This falls into the category of "stuff in flux on Facebook that may change soon," but for now, there's a neat trick you can use to quickly build up your fan base. In a nutshell, it involves advertising to places that already have proven to show a high affinity for your page. Let's take it a step at a time.

Step 1: Change from "You" on Facebook to Your Page

If you are the admin of a page, Facebook now gives you the option to assume the identity of that page. In other words, you can post comments on other pages under the name of your page. Making this shift can get interesting when it comes to advertising.

For example, I'm an admin of the page Left Action. Normally, when I log in I see the feed for me, John Hlinko, the person. I see updates from friends, suggested friends, suggested pages, and ads targeting me. But if I go to "Account," click "Use Facebook as Page" and click "Left Action," everything changes, and I'm now seeing a different view targeted toward the page. Most important, Facebook shows me pages that are popular with my fans.

Step 2: Gather Information on the "Recommended Pages"

In the case of Left Action specifically, out of roughly 102,000 Left Action fans, Facebook tells me that 14,767 are also fans of MoveOn.org, 9,550 are fans of the NPR show *Wait Wait . . . Don't Tell Me!*, 9,248 are fans of Planned Parenthood, 9,709 are fans of the TV show *Weeds*, and 9,825 are fans of Senator Bernie Sanders.

Note: Facebook doesn't actually present this information in a comprehensive list, rather it displays random selections of mutually popular pages on the side. The pages highlighted change each time, however, so if you refresh the page nine or ten times, you'll be able to get a list of about twenty or thirty of these pages. Make a list of them, including the number of their fans who like your page.

Step 3: Do a Page Affinity Analysis

What you're ultimately looking for is not just the raw numbers of that page's fans who like your page, but the *percentage* of those fans who like your page. Let's take the pages listed above with roughly the same number of fans who also like Left Action—in the nine thousands.

PAGE	TOTAL NUMBER OF FANS	FANS WHO LIKE LEFT ACTION	PERCENT WHO LIKE LEFT ACTION
Bernie Sanders	57,985	9,825	16.9%
Wait Wait Don't . . . Tell Me!	634,725	9,550	1.5%
Planned Parenthood	151,849	9,248	6.1%
Weeds	3,451,277	9,709	0.2%

While all of the pages have roughly the same raw number of fans who like Left Action, that stat alone is quite misleading. *Weeds*, a highly popular TV show, has over three million fans! So yes, it has a lot who like Left Action, but with those numbers, it will probably have a lot who like *any* page. Senator Bernie Sanders, on the other hand, has a far more concentrated group of fans, under sixty thousand. The fact that his page has produced over nine thousand crossover fans is far more significant, since it accounts for nearly 17 percent of his total!

Thus, we can reasonably conclude that while *Weeds* might have the same number of crossover fans, the fans of Bernie Sanders are far, far, far more likely *on average* to also have an affinity for Left Action. It's not surprising, since Left Action is a progressive activist community, and Bernie Sanders is a longtime progressive legislative leader. But then again, there are a number of progressive leaders in Congress. The fact that Bernie Sanders fans in particular have such an affinity is something we could only learn through this kind of analysis.

Step 4: Use the Data to Make Your Advertising Smarter

If we know that fans of Bernie Sanders have a far greater affinity for Left Action than fans of *Weeds*, we can also conclude the following:

- **They will be far more likely to click on Left Action ads.**

- **They will be far more likely to also become fans of Left Action once they get to the page.**

The higher your click-through rate, the lower Facebook will demand as payment per click. Therefore, if we target our ads toward fans of Bernie Sanders, we will be able to pay less plus get more fans, which equals awesome.

In order to do this targeting, enter the page name, in this case, "Bernie Sanders" in the "interests" section when you place the ad.

Your best bet will be to try this with a few ads, targeting fans of different pages that show up with high affinity ratings. Based on my experience advertising for myself and for clients, the higher the affinity rating, the better the results, and the greater your ability to get the most from your advertising dollars.

PEER PRESSURE

As with pages, Facebook now shows friends who like a page on ads for that page as well.

If you see an ad for a page, and friends like it, their names will show up right on the ad. Pretty compelling. And given that a one in one thousand click-through rate is considered good, even a teeny increase in the chance that I'll click could pay big dividends.

WHEN IT COMES TO ADVERTISING, there simply is no better venue than Facebook for targeting with such precision and still reaching a critical mass. If you are planning to advertise, Facebook should definitely be a part of your effort.

NINETEEN

"Echo Echo": Critical Mass Advertising

Thus far, we've talked about advertising in the traditional context—as a tool to get people to do something, whether it be visit a site, become a Facebook page fan, buy a product, or even spread the word.

If you want to get really creative with your advertising, however, you can also think of it as a tool to spur an "echo effect," one that is focused in a way aimed at reaching a critical mass and creating an explosion of viralization, awareness, and action.

THE ECHO EFFECT

By "echo effect," I don't just mean having people talk about your advertising because it's creative or funny. That's enormously important as well, of course. If you're trying to develop a message to be read and spread, there's no reason you can't do the same with your advertising as well.

An echo effect aimed at creating a critical mass, however, is a little different. The goal here isn't just to have people talking, it's to have them talking in a concentrated place, so that the echo is more likely to bounce back and forth in front of the same bystanders, forcing them to actually pay attention—and ideally start echoing it themselves.

We're actually talking about an "echo echo."

In more concrete terms, this means spurring conversations about the ad or its message around the watercooler or the virtual watercooler (a blog, a Facebook page, etc.). If one person says, "Hey, did you see that ad with . . . ," you want as many others as possible to answer yes, so the conversation can continue, rather than fizzle out.

This is exactly what can make your ads especially effective. If the person viewing your ad has already heard of the thing being advertised, even fleetingly, they are more likely to click on it to learn more. If they have heard of it in a positive way from a friend or other trusted source, they are much more likely to view it favorably themselves, thanks to the power of peer pressure.

Some campaigns, of course, can afford to make the whole country (or even the globe) their echo chamber. If you're spending tens of millions of dollars on a campaign, you may be among those fortunate few. For most of us working with far more limited budgets, however, creating an echo effect that leads to critical mass means focusing our efforts in a much more concentrated fashion.

USING FACEBOOK TO CREATE AN ECHO ECHO

Right now, Facebook is probably the best place to deploy a critical mass strategy cost effectively, given its size and the incredible ability to target. Here are some steps you can try.

Target by Geography

When you place an ad on Facebook, you have the option to target by state or city. So unless you have a specific reason for needing to go nationwide right away, try going local first. Try a few test ads with different cities, see what works best, and then pump a bunch into it. You may have no particular reason to push your product in Des Moines, Cincinnati, or Bismarck, but if you have no reason not to, get focused, and you'll increase the chances of stirring up conversation in a specific area.

Target by Workplace or School

This might be even better, since you'd be hitting a smaller community than a full-on city, and one far more likely to be connected already via email, intranets, or other online communities.

Try Targeting People Who Are Already Fans of Another Page That Is Logically Complementary to Yours

You can do this by typing in the name of the other page in the "interests" category when you place the ad (note, this doesn't always work, especially if the page is small). For example, if you're starting a page for your new wine shop, maybe target fans of a nearby high-end cheese shop. If you're lucky, fans who see your ad will start chatting about your new place on that page as well.

TO TEST WHETHER YOU'RE GETTING an echo effect with the ads, watch the click-through rate and see what happens over time. Facebook ads normally show a slow decrease in the click-through rate over time. This is primarily because the low-hanging fruit, those most likely to click, will generally do it when they first see the ad. If they haven't clicked by the fifth, tenth, or hundredth time they've seen it, odds are they're never going to click. Thus, the click-through rate should go down. Now, if it does go down, this doesn't necessarily mean you should kill the ad. It might still be working as an effective ad, it just isn't generating an echo effect.

On the other hand, if you really have created chatter, you might see the opposite. Let's say you're targeting a company of ten thousand people. On day one, your ads are just that—ads. But if you've got an echo going, by day two, three, or four, the people seeing it should start to see the names of coworkers who like the ad, and the underlying company, product, or cause. If you're lucky, they've started to talk about it via email, intranet, or even over the watercooler. And if *that* happens, by the time day five or six rolls around, and someone sees the ad, they might think, "Hey, that's that thing I've been hearing about. I should check that out."

If you do see a gradual increase in click-through rates, that's a pretty rare thing, and a good sign that some of the echo echo effect is happening.

OTHER ADVERTISING VENUES FOR CREATING AN ECHO ECHO

Facebook might offer the best venue for creating an echo echo effect, given its micro-targeting ability, but there are other ones you can take advantage of as well.

Using Blog Ads

Blogs are a good venue for this type of effort, given that conversation is built right into the structure. Thus, if you want to spur chatter, it can happen right then and there. Further, blogs also typically attract a far higher level of return visitors than normal websites. In part, this is because they are regularly updated, and people get in the habit of returning for more. Even more important, however, are the communities that they spawn. The chance to see and chat (or argue) with the same people is a powerful lure for people to return. Thus, you have a great combination—the ability to chat right there and the partners to chat with right there as well.

We've already covered in Chapter 17 the use of blog ads to insert yourself into the conversation, but you can take this a step further.

First, try concentrating your ads, to really break through the din. Rather than spreading out your buy across a whole range of blogs, focus in on one or two. Next, consider placing a few ads on the same blog, to really take it over. It may sound crazy to double or triple your effort on the same blog, but you're far more likely to spur conversation that way (even if it's just people asking, "Hey, what's the deal with the three ads from the same advertiser?").

Finally, if you've got enough of an ad budget, consider advertising on several blogs logically targeting the same area. If you're promoting your new book of wine and cheese recipes, for example, consider hitting several blogs in the "wine blogger" network at BlogAds.com. Many blog visitors with an interest in a specific category tend to hit a few blogs regularly, not just one. By hitting them with an ad in a few places, you increase the odds that they'll think the ad is everywhere and feel provoked to raise it as a topic of conversation with others.

Focused Ad Venues

Keep an eye out for other advertising venues that enable you to focus your ad on a small, concentrated community. The online versions of college newspapers, for example, can be a great place to reach a focused (and highly viral) group.

Many local communities also have online newspapers that are focused and generate nice chatter. If you're advertising in a big city, however, make sure to focus in on a community within it. Advertising on WashingtonPost.com, for example, might make sense in general, but given that it has an enormous number of readers in Washington and beyond, you're unlikely to create a concentrated echo. The *Georgetown Patch* or the *Georgetowner*, on the other hand, might be a lot more effective, given the focus on a specific neighborhood.

As always, make sure to compare prices across options, as some of these focused venues charge rates way out of proportion to their actual readership or page views.

WHEN CRAFTING AN ADVERTISING PLAN, make sure first and foremost to focus on what makes sense for reaching your target audience and getting them to do what it is that you want them to do. But recognize as well that advertising can also be "read and spread," and that if it effectively creates echoes of echoes, an ensuing critical mass can spur viralization that takes your advertising to a whole new level.

TWENTY

PR: Getting Reporters to Share Your Story

We've talked thus far about reaching individuals, with the goal of getting them to spread your message. But remember, there is an entire profession dedicated to spreading messages—reporters. Reporters are people who spend their waking hours in a constant search for spread-worthy stories to share with their readers, listeners, and viewers.

Regardless of where you are or what you're doing, the odds are that you can find reporters interested in your story—if you make it spread-worthy. Reporters cover all kinds of areas and have beats ranging from global to national to neighborhood. If you can find and engage the right ones, they can multiply your message, big-time.

BUILDING YOUR PR PLAN

The process of outreach to reporters is generally called public relations, or PR for short. At its heart, a good PR effort is fairly straightforward and consists of the following steps:

- **Decide who you want to reach (your end audience).**

- **Determine which reporters are creating content that reaches that audience.**

- **Come up with truly interesting things to say ("news").**

- **Pitch the reporters.**

- **Refine and repeat.**

Decide Who You Want to Reach

Think of the target audience bio you put together back in Chapter 2 and remind yourself of who it is that is ultimately the target. Male versus female, age range, location, interests, and whether they're confined to a specific geographic location.

Once you've determined your ideal target audience, the next step is to figure out what media sources they're likely to be reading/watching/listening to, when they're most likely to be thinking about what you want to sell them. For example, let's say you're selling baseball caps, and you've determined that men eighteen to thirty are your sweet spot. Of course, you could come up with a whole slew of media sources that they gravitate to, like *Sports Illustrated*, *Playboy*, *Maxim*, and ESPN. But a few of those clearly jump out as the more logical place to sell baseball caps, right? Your goal is not just to reach your audience but to reach them in a context in which they're willing, ready, and perhaps even eager to hear your message.

How can you come up with such a list? Hire a high-priced PR firm.

Oh, you can't afford that? No problem. Use your friend Google.

Come up with a list of logical keywords (your product category, your company/organization name, competitors), search Google News, and see what media sources pop up as covering it regularly. Then add the relevant ones to your media outreach list. If you were selling baseball caps, for example, search for mentions of names of other companies that sell them as well, in addition to terms like "baseball caps" or "baseball hats" or "baseball uniforms."

Next, try the same with blogs. Not only do some of them get astonishingly high levels of traffic, the fact that they're online makes them a wonderful complement to your other online efforts. (If someone is reading about you on a blog, they're just a few clicks away from tweeting, sharing, or emailing the information to someone else.) Google has a blogs search option that works pretty well for this.

Next, move on to Facebook pages. Hey, some of these have tens or hundreds of thousands of fans. Some have millions. Why not pitch them too? Search on Facebook for relevant pages, and find the contacts for the admins. This can be a little tricky, since while some Facebook pages list the admin, making contact easy, most still do not (it's a new, optional feature). Thus, you might need to dig through a few posts to see if he/she mentions his/her name.

Prioritize

After you've built your list, prioritize. Generally, this means the bigger the audience, the better. Use your judgment, but if you're targeting Facebook pages, for example, prioritize the ones with the most fans. Targeting blogs or online news outlets? Go for the ones with more traffic.

Some media sources will actually publish such data, while others may not. Within the PR industry, there are sources that track this as well (usually for a fee). However, if you want a good, simple way to gauge orders of magnitude, check their websites' reach by using Compete.com. This is a site where you can go, enter a URL, and find out how much traffic a site gets and has gotten over time. It's not 100 percent precise, but you don't need 100 percent precise.

Note: You can use this approach for TV, radio, or print outlets as well to guesstimate their reach (that is, use whatever website they have, even if it's not their main focus). Granted, it might seem a little odd to judge TV channels by their website traffic, but given how mature the web has become, it's at least a decent proxy for non-web traffic.

Finally, for blogs, I find BlogAds.com to be a wonderful source for determining blog traffic. Not all blogs are listed there, of course, but thousands are. If you want to get a sense of how big a blog is, it's worth checking BlogAds.com, to see if they're there. If they are, you'll get page views per week for each, right to the exact number.

Get Familiar with Reporters

Once you have your sources identified, you'll want to figure out which reporters at those sources actually cover what you want to pitch. The last thing you want is to be the guy sending press releases to "Editor" or some other generic recipient. The odds are slim that such press releases will ever get read.

Again, Google can be your friend. See what articles have been written, and see what reporters are attached to them. Look for reporters who have done several stories and get to know their style, what motivates them, and what kind of stories they like, as that will come in handy later.

Once you have your list of reporters, you'll want to get their contact info. Your mileage may vary, as different reporters like to be contacted in different ways, but you'll ideally want to track down as much of the following as possible:

- **EMAIL: Probably the best way to contact most reporters these days, since it lets them respond when they have a minute and also lets you include links to websites or Facebook pages with more information.**

- **TELEPHONE:** Some folks still like the personal touch of a phone call, and some folks are frankly caught off guard and forced to respond (as opposed to email, which they might ignore).

- **FACEBOOK AND TWITTER CONTACTS:** A huge number of reporters are on Facebook and Twitter, and many of them respond more quickly to a message sent via those channels. And for reaching Facebook admins, of course, this is a natural.

You can often get contact info for them from the articles themselves, as many include email links. If not, you can try searching Google for logical possibilities. Try their name plus "email" and see what comes up. Or try their first initial, last name, and domain (for example, JSmith@NYtimes.com) and see if results pop up. And there's nothing wrong with actually emailing or calling the publication to see if they'll give you the reporter's contact info.

Come Up with Truly Interesting Things to Say ("News")

Sounds obvious, right? Yet, every day, reporters are overwhelmed by eminently crappy pitches about astonishingly boring things. Generally, these are pitches where the pitcher is focused on "information they need to get out" as opposed to "stuff that will be interesting to the reporter and his/her audience."

Use the tactics we've already discussed to come up with stories that are interesting, awesome, and spread-worthy. Beyond that, make sure to come up with spins that are new, since that is what reporters actually cover. For example, if you're pitching your wine store, the fact that you have one isn't particularly newsworthy in itself. Figure out a hook. A local reporter might cover a tenth anniversary party, or a reporter with an environmental hook might cover the fact that you're making all red and white wine "green wine" by planting a tree for each bottle sold.

Do you have something fun to say? Even if your news isn't particularly interesting, can you spin it in a fun or comedic way? Reporters know that their readers and viewers enjoy humor (who doesn't?), and a comedic hook might be the touch of spice that makes the story interesting. Back in 2003, I ran a campaign to draft General Wesley Clark to run for president. We decided it would be fun to hand out Clark bars, a chocolate bar that coincidentally had the same name. That silly (but fun) little stunt managed to get coverage from CNN—twice—as well as a slew of other TV and print venues. The serious story, the draft effort, came along for the ride.

Having a sale at your bakery? Not terribly interesting or newsworthy. But remember the "Rickroll" example from Chapter 8? The offer of free rolls to anyone who sang the Rick Astley song in the bakery? That's actually one of the silly but fun hooks that reporters enjoy, because they know their readers will enjoy it as well.

Finally, before you pitch, put the news in a release or other easily digestible, understandable format. Some say the press release is outdated, but the reality is a one-pager that is basically written like a short article is still a nicely packaged form for a reporter.

Use the following format:

- **A catchy headline that gives the big hook (like a newspaper headline). Traditional press releases put this below the contact info, but since you're likely going to be sending this via email rather than fax, as in the past, I'd recommend getting the hook up top.**

- **Your contact info just below it (name, organization, telephone, and email). If you have a website address in it (or in the text below), make sure to include the "http://" at the beginning so they're clickable if emailed.**

- **A three-hundred- to five-hundred-word story, written like a newspaper article (but of course, an _absolutely glowing_ one).**

- **Key points all highlighted up top, in the first paragraph or two.**

- **A few juicy quotes that the reporter could lift verbatim.**

For example, here's what you might use for the bakery "Rick-roll" press release:

TASTIEST "RICKROLL" EVER? ENZO'S BAKERY OFFERS FREE ROLL TO ANYONE WHO SINGS RICK ASTLEY SONG IN PERSON!

Contact: Enzo Parrilli
Enzo@EnzosFamilyBaker.com
Tel: 212-555-1212
http://EnzosFamilyBakery.com

(New York, NY: May 31, 2012)—Enzo's Family Bakery, a New York family favorite since 1922, today announced the "tastiest Rickroll ever," offering a free hot roll to any customer who comes into the store this Friday between noon and one and sings the Rick Astley song "Never Gonna Give You Up."

"Rickrolling has been fun for years, but never before has it been so delicious," said owner Enzo Parrilli. "For all those who've been Rickrolled or who've Rickrolled someone else, we're never gonna give you up—we're just gonna give you the tastiest rolls in New York."

The baker's offer is a play on "Rickrolling," the practice of . . . etc.

The release should go on to give some more background, the address, and add another quote. But really, once you've got the big hook up top, you've got 90 percent of the value.

Don't be afraid to get a bit edgy. Remember, assume the reporter is getting this as the 118th email in their inbox. What makes it interesting?

Here, for example, is the press release we issued for the "Just Say Blow" effort described in Chapter 9:

STUDENTS FOR A DRUG-FREE WHITE HOUSE LAUNCHES RADIO AD CAMPAIGN AGAINST BUSH POLICY DENYING FUNDS TO THOSE WITH DRUG PASTS

(OAKLAND, Calif., Jun. 20, 2001)—Students for a Drug-Free White House today launched its first radio ad campaign to support its "JustSayBlow.com" online petition effort. The ad will begin airing this week in selected markets, including Coke, Texas; Powderhorn, Colo.; and Blowville, Ohio. It was also emailed to more than 6,000 Just Say Blow petition supporters today, and is posted for listening and downloading at www .JustSayBlow.com/radio. CDs are available for college stations and others who wish to air it as a public service announcement. The group is combating a Bush Administration policy denying aid to students who refuse to answer . . .

In one fell swoop, we quickly go their attention by creating a problem ("Wait, students for a drug-free White House? Isn't that backward?"), making it clear that this would be fun and funny (note the names of the cities), and also establishing credibility (six thousand petition supporters, a respectable number, especially for 2001).

Pitch the Reporters

Make sure you're familiar with a few examples of what a reporter has done when you pitch them. Reporters are people too, and most are flattered when you refer to their past work. Alternatively, if you appear clueless about their past work, it's a sign that you don't have the respect for them to take even a few minutes to research said work. Now, it doesn't mean they're going to write nice things about you because you were nice to them. But it might mean that they're at least more willing to give a fair hearing. You've shown them respect, and that (maybe) might convince them you're worth some respect yourself. This goes for blogs as well. It might just be one or two people doing the whole thing, but getting their names is generally pretty easy, either from the site or from Google, and using it is a sign of respect (small thing, but small things matter).

Think of ways to customize the pitch for each reporter. What facet of what you have to say will be of most interest to them?

How should you deliver the pitch? Yes, this takes time to customize for each reporter, but if you take that time, your odds of success will jump quite a bit. If you're pitching your baseball cap story, for example, a business reporter might be interested in the company story (sales, profits, and growth), while a sports reporter might be more interested in which team's hats sold the most. The latter example isn't as crazy as it sounds. I had one client, Cafe Press.com, that sells political shirts and hats and got a lot of press during the 2008 election with a meter that constantly displayed which candidate for president was ahead in sales at that moment. It was a new, fresh measure of momentum, one that reporters found a welcome relief from the constant onslaught of polls, polls, and more polls.

Make sure to get feedback from the reporter. If they like the pitch, find out why. If they don't, find out why. Be respectful of their time and realize that they might be juggling twenty other pitches at the same time, but even a few seconds of feedback can help you better customize your pitch for the next time (or alternatively, realize that they're not worth pitching).

Whatever you do, make sure to track the feedback and use it to improve your outreach accordingly over time. Reporters work hard (well, most of them), and they do appreciate it when you make their jobs easier. Giving them good stories and being attuned to their unique needs *makes their jobs easier.*

Lather, Rinse, Repeat

Okay, you've crafted a great story, you've pitched it to a hundred reporters, and 90 percent hang up on you, never answer your email, or tell you it's not of interest to them.

Guess what? You did great! If you can honestly get 10 percent of reporters to at least be interested in your story, then chances are you'll get a couple of them to actually cover your story. And that's great. Even if you didn't get a reporter to cover you, at least you've started to build a relationship and set the stage for the next possible pitch.

INTEGRATING YOUR PR EFFORT WITH THE REST OF YOUR MARKETING EFFORT

There are a number of steps you can take to create a (buzzword warning) "synergistic" effect—that is, one in which your target audience is hearing your message from multiple fronts, and thus amplifying the impact.

Synch Up Timing and Location

This may sound obvious, but it's often overlooked. If you're going to be doing paid marketing and PR, make sure to synch up the timing between the efforts. A great, compelling Facebook ad might draw a nice number of clicks from your target audience. But guess what? It'll draw even more clicks if the viewer just happens to have read an article or blog post about you just before that. If you're going to be doing PR and paid marketing, try to synch things up so your marketing is hitting just as your earned media stories are.

The same goes for location. Facebook, for example, will let you target your ads by geographic location. Going to be making a PR splash in Cincinnati? Ramp up your Facebook ads and other paid marketing targeting the people there!

Cross-Leverage Back and Forth Between Paid and Earned Media

Doing well on one front can provide a proof point for the other. For example, let's say you get a wonderful article in a prominent newspaper or magazine, or better yet, a wonderful story on TV. Consider doing the following:

- **Post the article in a prominent place on your website. Seeing a great hit gives you validation for site visitors. People who visit will be more likely to sign up if they see a news article validating your credibility (and frankly, confirming you're not a scam). Not all articles are equal. Many folks default to a rather dumb "news page" format that simply lists all articles in reverse chronological** order. But remember, you're not trying to inform them here, you're trying to *influence* them.

- Put it out on Twitter, via email, or a Facebook post. You won't want to put out every article, of course, and you'll want to respect the optimal frequencies of communication for each of these platforms. But if you get a great hit, go ahead and share it! This is the kind of thing that excites your supporters and makes them feel they're part of something successful. And of course, this is the kind of thing they might share with others, which is really the point, right?

On the flip side, let's say you've gained some real traction on the paid marketing front and you've built up some newsworthy metrics. This can in fact be a good story in itself and worthy of a press release. "Wow, in just forty-eight hours since our official launch of the new Facebook fan page for our baseball cap made from recycled cow dung, we've already got five thousand fans!"

FUN (AND EFFECTIVE) TRICKS

Above and beyond the tactics above, there are a number of additional fun tricks you can use on the PR front. Here are a few to consider:

"Coincidental Call"

Some email systems will actually allow you to track when individual recipients have opened an email and when they've clicked on a link. So . . . if you email a list of reporters, it would make sense to "coincidentally" call them to follow up, just as you've seen them open and/or click on a link in your email. It's not a guarantee of anything, but hey, if you hit them when they're actually at least fleetingly engaged with your pitch, you're more likely to get a willing ear.

Ads That Appear to Be "Everywhere"

Run Facebook ads that look generally focused but are actually targeting your reporters. Facebook lets you target by workplace. Great! Just make those workplaces CNN, ESPN, the *New York Times*, or whatever media outlet is relevant. Your ad will now start showing up when they're on Facebook (and frankly, most are these days), and they'll either end up clicking on it (good!), or at the very least feeling like they've "seen you before" when you pitch them. Again, don't make it overtly directed at them ("Hey, you reporters, cover this story . . ."), make it a generally targeted ad they "happen" to see.

WHEN IT COMES TO GETTING your message spread, there are no bigger multipliers than reporters. Do your research, target appropriately, give them something spread-worthy, and your reward might be a message spread to thousands, hundreds of thousands, or even millions.

TWENTY-ONE

Overcoming the "Joy Sponges"

You've learned how the technology works. You've learned who the right people are to reach, if you want your message to be spread. You've learned how to craft the perfect message. You're ready to go!

Until, that is, some "joy sponge" tries to stop you.

Who are the joy sponges? They are the bane of your existence if you're trying to implement something the least bit creative, interesting, spread-worthy, and different from everything that's gone before.

Nearly every great idea has to contend with the joy sponges. You've seen them. You might be sitting around a table of ten people, brainstorming ideas for a marketing campaign. Someone comes up with a brilliant, creative, and yes, edgy campaign. One that really is awesome. Nine of the ten people at the table howl with laughter. But the tenth one frowns, insisting that "someone" might be offended by the idea. Not them. Not anyone they can name. But "someone." This tenth person is the dreaded joy sponge, the one who literally soaks the joy out of the room. And yet, invariably, it is the one joy sponge that so often can overwhelm the other nine supporters, water down a great idea, and leave the world just a little more . . . joyless.

WHY THE JOY SPONGES USUALLY WIN

Why is it that one joy sponge so often can overrule nine or ten others ready to take a risk? Simply put, no one ever got fired for playing it safe. Well, very few people, at least. But a heck of a lot more people have lost their jobs for taking a risk—even a sensible one. That's the real problem with the joy sponges. Because as we've seen, the best, more spread-worthy messages are exactly the ones that are most creative, novel, and problem-causing.

Think of some of the ideas we've examined already. Take the Whopper Sacrifice in Chapter 10, for example, the one that offered free Whoppers in exchange for de-friending people on Facebook. That's exactly the kind of idea that would've freaked out a joy sponge. I can picture it now:

> JOY SPONGE: We're asking people to de-friend friends? Won't that be . . . offensive to some?
>
> SENSIBLE PERSON: Yes. And funny to about one hundred times as many others, which is why it will spread like wildfire.
>
> JOY SPONGE: Yes, true . . . but maybe we should play it safe.
>
> SENSIBLE PERSON: And maybe you should stick your head up your butt and keep pushing until you completely disappear.

Okay, I'm guessing that didn't actually happen, since Crispin (the ad agency behind it) had a string of wildly creative successful campaigns and probably managed to minimize their joy sponge contingent. Then again, joy sponges seem to termite their way into pretty much everywhere, so . . . who knows.

Most often, the joy sponges end up killing a good idea because it's simply a little edgy, and thus comes with some risk, even a teeny, weeny, almost imperceptible one. Ideally, such risk should be sensibly compared with the potential reward, and a decision made in a rational way by weighing the two. Sure, it's worrisome if a few hundred people might be offended by something you send, and unsubscribe from your email list or Facebook page. But if a few thousand people end up joining because of the resultant viral spreading, that's certainly a net gain, right? All too often, however, good ideas never get to that test phase, and instead die in the brainstorm phase. Someone (joy sponge) raises an objection, everyone pauses, no one rises to defend it, and the idea dies.

DEFEATING THE JOY SPONGES

Remember Seth Godin's purple cow metaphor? How regular cows get lost in the herd? How purple cows, on the other hand, stand out, get noticed, and generate a whole lot of buzz? Purple cows are exactly what joy sponges are on the lookout for. "Normal cow, normal cow, normal cow . . . purple cow? Get me my shotgun!"

That's the crux of the problem. It's not just that joy sponges are going after ideas in a random pattern—they are going after the ideas most likely to perform most effectively in a viral world. If your great idea is the virus, they are the virus killer. The "cure" that you're absolutely not looking for when you want to create spread-worthy campaigns.

You will face this challenge at some point. You will have a great idea; some joy sponge will try to kill it. Here's how you'd probably like to react in the situation:

> **YOU:** . . . And so it turns out that the man would not in fact be a man, but . . . a rhesus monkey in a tuxedo!

EVERYONE ELSE: Wow! That's brilliant! I love it, would totally spread that, and I bet everyone else would! Viral firestorm, here we come!

JOY SPONGE: Yeah, it's great, but . . . what about people who like spider monkeys and not rhesus monkeys? Wouldn't they be offended?

YOU: Do you actually know anyone who'd be offended?

JOY SPONGE: Well, no, but I think we're better off not risking it, just in case. Let's play it safe, and just use (insert crappy idea here that won't work).

YOU: I hate you with every fiber of my being. You are a soulless destroyer of all that is new, joyful, and effective. I will now have you terminated. That sound you hear? That is Captain Kirk and the crew of the USS *Enterprise*, beaming into the room as we speak, ready to reduce you to space dust.

CAPTAIN KIRK, SPOCK, AND RANDOM SECURITY GUARDS APPEAR, PUT PHASERS ON "KILL," AND INSTANTLY VAPORIZE THE JOY SPONGE. YOU ARE HELD ALOFT BY YOUR COLLEAGUES AS THEY ENTHUSIASTICALLY CELEBRATE THE END OF THE JOY SPONGE'S TYRANNICAL REIGN.

That's how I'd like to play it out, at least. But for a host of reasons, it's just not practical. William Shatner, for example, is doing multiple TV shows right now, and would be tough to get.

Fortunately, you don't need to go to these lengths. This is the world where the Internet reigns supreme, and one in which data is very easy to come by. And data will help you prove your point quickly and easily. Try this version instead:

JOY SPONGE: Let's play it safe, and just use (insert crappy idea here that won't work).

YOU: You may be right. But how about we just do a tiny pilot version, try my idea to a small subset of the list, try yours as well, and see what works better? It'll just be a pilot version. Just a test. What say you?

It's important to get the word "test" in there. Who can be opposed to "testing" an idea? Science is good, right? You'll sound smart, and you'll be smart. Even if you don't win over the joy sponge, coming across as the sensible "science-y" one will help you win over your colleagues.

At that point, you'll be ready to use any number of the methods described in this book to test the ideas side by side. Just set up criteria first for what defines "success," and measure both accordingly. This might be as simple as two emails sent to 5 percent of your list to see which generates the most click-throughs, opens, and spreading.

Once you have the test results for the "pilot," you can actually talk data, rather than spend hours with each side arguing by hunch or by anecdote. And if your idea has been proven to be the superior one, it'll be a heck of a lot easier to get your colleagues and boss to run with it.

Sometimes you'll face a particularly tough joy sponge, one that really "sucks" to an extraordinary degree and who will combat even the idea of a test. They might fret, for example, that "the test one might get out beyond the test audience, and spread to those who might be offended!" (And of course, your whole point is to create viral-worthy content, so it's hard to squelch this objection out of hand.) If you face this, here are a few other approaches to try to defuse the joy sponges:

- **Point out something equal or more edgy that a competitor is doing:** Remember the Asch experiment cited in Chapter 1 about the astonishing power of peer pressure? It holds not just for individuals but companies and organizations as well. Most live in constant fear of competitors, and most (foolishly) assume that these same competitors never make decisions that are not in their own best interest. If you show an example of a competitor doing something edgy, the reactions will likely be "Well, that must be a good idea" and "Holy crap, we'd better catch up!"

- Push the argument toward tangible goals and measures, as opposed to hunches, fears, and opinions. Without this, and debates just based on what you "feel," well, heck, you might as well be arguing about religion. And we all know how well *those* arguments end.

- Argue each other's opinion. Spend five minutes each, arguing why the other guy is right. Even if you don't really believe it, it's amazing how effective this can be in forcing oneself to at least break out of one's opinion long enough to see the light of the other guy's position. With luck, your joy sponge might at least soften his or her position enough to agree to a "pilot" or "test."

If all else fails, make 100 percent sure to at least get "I told you so" points. Stake out a position, make your case, and if you're lucky, you'll have the chance to push your point the next time around, once it's abundantly clear that the joy sponge's approach has been an abysmal failure.

TWENTY-TWO

Putting It All Together

The world has changed, the rules have changed, and the power of viral marketing means that the little guy now has the power to spread a message as never before.

With hard work, creativity, and an understanding of what these new rules are, you really can make this happen. I've seen it before. We've all seen it before. MoveOn.org, an online effort that has redefined grassroots activism, was launched by a couple from their house. Facebook, one of the hottest and most valuable companies on the planet, was started by one guy from his dorm room. And every day, as we speak, some new effort from a "little guy" is morphing into the next mega-hot company or social revolution.

What is your goal? It may be to be the next entrepreneur who launches a billion-dollar idea. Or it may simply be to get more exposure for an effort that is much smaller in scope, but still very important to you personally. Either way, your path to that goal will be easier and more efficient if you can harness the power of the Viral Trifecta, and understand its three components—message, messengers, and mechanism—as thoroughly as possible.

Once you've done that, and you're ready to get started, here's my parting advice for moving forward:

JUST GET STARTED

It sounds so simple, and yet, all too many people spend forever thinking about great ideas but never pulling the trigger. Set a goal, set a deadline, and then take your first step. It may be setting up a Facebook page, building a website, or crafting the perfect humorous marketing pitch. But whatever it is, just make it happen—and then move on to the second step, and all the steps beyond.

STRIVE TO FAIL TEN TIMES

I'm serious. Many people spend an insane amount of time trying to craft the perfect home-run idea, and waste all their time and resources pushing as hard as possible on that one and that one alone. Be creative, work hard, and give it your best shot. But also recognize that some of the path to success involves luck, and even more of the path involves making mistakes and learning from them. In my own case, I've now reached a point where I can routinely launch a Facebook page and attract tens of thousands of fans with no marketing budget. But I only got there after having built many, many other pages that never attracted more than a few dozen fans. It's failures that serve as the foundation for your subsequent successes. So strive to fail ten times, do it as quickly as possible, and I'm willing to bet number eleven will be a success.

BE DATA DRIVEN

The great advantage of an online-driven effort is the vast amount of data that it generates—in real time. The great tragedy is that so many marketers end up ignoring this data, and either shooting from the hip or talking themselves into a direction that *they* love, even if their target audience doesn't. Let the data be your guide. Once you've figured out your goal, figure out what specific pieces of data prove whether or not you are moving toward it, and watch that data like a hawk.

And if you fail? Use the data to figure out why.

IGNORE THE NAYSAYERS

As you strive to make an impact, many naysayers will try to hold you back. Some will be the joy sponges, the ones so scared of their own shadows that they will try to squelch any idea with the least bit of edginess. Some naysayers will be scared of anything new, especially involving technology. And some will simply be people who haven't the least bit of ambition and simply feel more comfortable when those around them are dragged down to their level. Don't let them do it. Don't let the naysayers win.

YOU'VE GOT THE TOOLS, YOU'VE got the knowledge, and you're poised to launch a revolution.

Now it's time to just get started.

ENDNOTES

1. THE FIERCE URGENCY OF GOING VIRAL

1. Facebook, "Statistics": www.facebook.com/press/info.php?statistics.
2. Charles Arthur, "Average Twitter User Has 126 Followers, and Only 20% of Users Go Via Website," *Guardian* (UK), June 29, 2009: www.guardian.co.uk/technology/blog/2009/jun/29/twitter-users-average-api-traffic.
3. Christina Warren, "Average Internet User Now Spends 68 Hours per Month Online," *Mashable*, October 14, 2009: http://mashable.com/2009/10/14/net-usage-nielsen.
4. "What Americans Do Online: Social Media and Games Dominate Activity," Nielsen Wire, August 2, 2010: http://blog.nielsen.com/nielsenwire/online_mobile/what-americans-do-online-social-media-and-games-dominate-activity.
5. Tom Johansmeyer, "200 Million Twitter Accounts . . . But How Many Are Active?" *Social Times*, February 3, 2011: http://socialtimes.com/200-million-twitter-accounts-but-how-many-are-active_b36952.
6. Greg Kumparak, "Friendster: Asia's Social Network," *TechCrunch*, January 20, 2009: http://techcrunch.com/2009/01/20/friendster-asias-social-network. Also Wikipedia lists dozens of other sites at http://en.wikipedia.org/wiki/List_of_social_networking_websites.
7. S. E. Asch, "Studies of Independence and Conformity: A Minority of One Against a Unanimous Majority," *Psychological Monographs* 70 (1956). Also "Asch conformity experiments," Wikipedia: http://en.wikipedia.org/wiki/Asch_conformity_experiments for more details.
8. "Yes We Can," Wikipedia: http://en.wikipedia.org/wiki/Yes_We_Can.

5. USING FACEBOOK

9. Erica Swallow, "5 Masterminds Redefining Social Media Marketing," *Mashable*, January 21, 2011: http://mashable.com/2011/01/21/social-media-marketing-masterminds/.

8. MAKING YOUR MESSAGE SPREAD-WORTHY

10. Personal interview, April 2011.

10. GIVING THEM A PROBLEM

11. Personal interview, March 2011.

12. Michael Arrington, "Facebook Blows a Whopper of an Opportunity," *TechCrunch*, January 14, 2009: http://techcrunch.com/2009/01/14/face book-blows-a-whopper-of-an-opportunity/.

11. USING SEX APPEAL

13. Lindsay Powers, "GQ: Racy 'Glee' Photos Are 'Gift That Keeps on Giving,'" *The Hollywood Reporter*, November 1, 2010: www.hollywoodreporter .com/news/gq-racy-glee-photos-are-34087.

14. Bryce Durbin, "HotOrNot Apparently Very Hot: Acquired for $20 Million," *TechCrunch*, February 11, 2008: http://techcrunch.com/2008/02/11/ hotornot-apparently-very-hot-acquired-for-20-million.

15. Chiara Atik, "Would You Let a Cab Driver Set You Up?" How About We . . . , February 15, 2011: www.howaboutwe.com/date-report/714 -would-you-let-a-cab-driver-set-you-up.

INDEX

Pages in **bold** indicate tables; those in *italics* indicate figures.

"about" page, websites, 37–38
"about" section, Facebook, 58
above/below the fold, 152–53, 154
ActForLove.org, 39, 92, 101, 113, 119, 168
action desired ("what") of target audience, 17, 19–20, 34
AddThis.com, 41, 42, 84
"admins," Facebook, 57
advertising, 147–89
  above/below the fold, 152–53, 154
  believability of, xiii
  click-through rates, 155, 160, 162, 165, 168, 169, 170, 182, 183, 186, 187
  clip art for, 149–50
  combination image and text ads, 151–52
  cost per click (CPC), 64, 153–54, 159, 162, 173, 174, 175, 178
  cost per thousand views (CPM), 64, 153, 154, 156, 165–66, 169, 173, 178
  crafting your ad, 162–63, 166–68
  echo effect, 184–89
  email and, 148, 155, 157, 158, 192, 193, 194, 195, 196, 197, 198, 200, 204, 206
  flexibility importance, 156
  focus on results, 147–49
  headlines, 57, 151, 160, 163, 166, 167–68, 174, 195
  hooks for, 148, 156–58
  image ads, 149–50, 152
  images in ads, 166, 167, 169, 175–76
  keywords, 77, 161, 165, 172
  links in, 160, 166–67
  measuring results, 148
  online medium focus, 148, 156
  optimizing ads, 163, 168–70, 178–79
  paying for advertising, 152–54
  placement of ads, 152–53
  places to advertise, choosing, 154–56
  plan for, 188–89
  prioritizing advertising, 148
  public relations (PR) and, 157, 158
  publishers, 150, 155–56
  radio advertising, 148, 158
  target audience ("who"), 155, 189
  testing, 154–55, 163, 168–70, 178–79, 186–87
  text ads, 150–51, 152, 159, 162–63, 174–75
  time duration, paying, 152–53, 154, 165–66
  TV advertising, 148, 156–57, 158
  Twitter and, 73, 76
  websites and, 148
  See also blogs advertising; Facebook advertising; Google AdWords; jump-starting marketing; spread-worthy content; viral marketing
Advertising Age, 17
African-American baseball players, 91
all-in-one back-end platforms, 31–32, 43–44, 48, 49
Amazon, xii, 105
American Society of Magazine Editors, 114
animal instincts, messages, 15, 28, 116–21

AOL, 52, 136
Apple "1984" ad, 14, 15, 95
apps (applications), Facebook, 66–67
Armisen, Fred, 101–2, 103, 132
Asch, Solomon, 10
Asch experiments, 10, *10*, 37, 206–7
Ashley Madison, 114
"Ass Clown of the Year" contest, 96
Astley, Rick, 94, 95, 195
automatic sub/unsubscribing email, 48

Badoo, 9
BarelyPolitical.com, 15
Bauman, Yoram, 92
Beatles, 4
believability of advertising, xiii
below the fold, 152–53, 154
Beyoncé, 6
bidding, 161, 178
BlackBerrys, 45
Black Eyed Peas, 12
Bleyer, Kevin, 101, 102
BlogAds.com
    advertising and, 151, 154, 156,
        164–65
    conversations and ads, 169–70,
        187–88
    optimizing ads, 168–69
    traffic activity, 193
    See also blogs; blogs advertising
blog-based platforms, websites, 32–33
Blogger.com, 33, 34–35
blogs, 81–86
    email and, 84
    "evergreen" content, 84
    Facebook and, 55, 82, 85
    frequency of posts, 82–83, 84
    jump-starting marketing, 185, 192,
        193, 197, 199
    links in, 83, 84, 85, 166–67
    media sources, finding, 192, 193
    messages (Viral Trifecta), 111
    messengers (Viral Trifecta),
        134, 138
    optimizing, 83–84
    recycling mode, 84, 86
    social media and, 84–86
    spread-worthy content, 82–84
    time for, 83, 86
    titles, optimizing for searching, 84
    tracking activity, 84
    Twitter and, 71, 82, 85–86
    uniform resource locators
        (URLs), 84
    updating content, 82–83, 84

viral marketing and, 11, 12, 13
websites and, 26, 29, 32, 33, 34, 35,
    81, 82, 84
See also BlogAds.com; blogs adver-
    tising; mechanism for delivery
    (Viral Trifecta); spread-worthy
    content; viral marketing
blogs advertising, 164–70, 187–88
    choosing blogs for, 165–66
    click-through rates, 165, 168,
        169, 170
    conversations and ads, 169–70,
        187–88
    cost per thousand views (CPM),
        165–66, 169
    crafting your ad, 166–68
    echo effect, 185, 187–88
    flexibility, 156
    headlines, 166, 167–68
    hives (subgroups of blogs), 165
    images in ads, 166, 167, 169
    Internet and, 164
    keywords, 165
    links in, 166–67
    optimizing ads, 168–70
    target audience ("who"), 170
    testing, 168–70
    time duration, paying, 165–66
    See also advertising; BlogAds.com;
        blogs
bookmarking, 41
Brady Bunch (TV show), 92
brands and signaling, 109–10
budget for Facebook advertising,
    64–65, 173, 177–78
Burger King, 110–12, 203
Bush, George W., 4–5, 91, 105–6, 158
Businessweek, 114

CafePress.com, 198
calendar events, riding existing
    wave, 93
Cheney, Dick, 95
Clark, Wesley (General), 50,
    156–57, 195
click, cost per (CPC), 64, 153–54, 159,
    162, 173, 174, 175, 178
click-through rates, 155, 160, 162, 165,
    168, 169, 170, 182, 183, 186, 187
Clinton, Hillary, 11, 13, 14
clip art, 35, 149–50
CNN, 85–86, 195, 201
cognitive dissonance, 112
coincidental call, 200
Coke, 17, 19

collecting data, websites, 42–43
combination image and text ads, 151–52
".com" domain name suffix, 26, 27
comments (soliciting) Facebook, 61, 63
communities, focused ad venues, 188
community building on Twitter, 71–73
Compete.com, 192–93
complementary pages, Facebook, 186
concrete goals, 18, 19
connections, Facebook, 55, 176–77
consultants, websites, 24–26, 30, 33–34, 41
contact information, 37, 38–39, 195
content. *See* spread-worthy content
contests, 64, 96
context and messengers, 132
conversations, blogs, 169–70, 187–88
Convio.com, 31, 48
cost per click (CPC), 64, 153–54, 159, 162, 173, 174, 175, 178
cost per thousand views (CPM), 64, 153, 154, 156, 165–66, 169, 173, 178
crafting your ad, 162–63, 166–68
Craigslist, 26
Crispin Porter & Bogusky, 109, 110, 111, 112, 203–4
critical mass advertising, 184–89
cross-leveraging marketing, 199–200
"Crush on Obama" (video), 14, 118
CSV file, 46
cultural references, riding existing wave, 93–94, 95
curling (sport), 93, 101
custom-built platforms, 30
"cynicism filter," email, 51
cynicism vs. humor in messages, 99

Daily Kos (blog), 12
Daily Show with Jon Stewart, The (TV show), 101, 102
databases, 31, 32, 43–44, 141
data driven viral marketing, 209–10
DC Cupcakes (TLC reality show), 80
"de-friending," Facebook, 111–12, 203
delivery. *See* mechanism for delivery (Viral Trifecta)
Democratic Party, 4, 11, 12, 13, 91, 95, 115, 167, 168
demographics of target audience, 18–19

Dennehy, Dennis, 94
designing websites, 24, 25, 26, 31, 33–36
de Vellis, Phil, 15
Dipdive.com, 12
Disney, xi
DNS settings, 28
Doby, Larry, 91
domain names, 26–28, 41, 57
Doodlekit.com, 33
download caution, 35, 51
DraftObama.org, xi
DraftWesleyClark.com, 156–57
DreamHost.com, 32–33
Drummond, Colin, 109, 110
Drupal.org, 30, 31, 32, 34

echo effect, 184–89
Edwards, John, 11
email, 45–54
    advertising and, 148, 155, 157, 158, 192, 193, 194, 195, 196, 197, 198, 200, 204, 206
    automatic sub/unsubscribing, 48
    blogs and, 84
    click-through rates, 128, 133
    coincidental call, 200
    cross-leveraging marketing, 200
    "cynicism filter," 51
    databases, 141
    download caution, 51
    exporting members, 46
    Facebook and, 45–46, 59, 60, 64, 186, 187
    frequency of, 49–50
    "from" line, 50
    grouping members, 46–47
    importing new members, 46
    jump-starting marketing, 193, 194, 196, 200
    links in, 43, 44, 48, 51, 133–34
    messages (Viral Trifecta), 96, 99, 100, 102, 104, 107, 113, 115, 119, 122–28
    messengers (Viral Trifecta), 132, 133–35, 136, 137, 138, 140, 141, 142, 143
    118th email test, 90, 196
    open rates, 127
    personalization, 47–48, 51
    public relations (PR) and, 51
    "scraped" emails, 39
    spam, 39, 48, 52–53
    spread-worthy content, 49–53, 124–28

email (*cont.*)
subgroups, sending to, 46–47
subject line, 50–51, 123, 126, 127
subscribing, 48
target audience ("who"), 104
testing, 51, 52–53, 90, 122–28,
142–43, 155
text vs. HTML, 51, 52
tracking activity, 48–49, 133–35,
136
Twitter and, 45–46, 77
unsubscribing, 48
updating records, 140–41
viral marketing and, 3, 5, 9, 13,
19, 20
websites and, 23, 31, 32, 33, 39, 41,
43, 44
See also mechanism for delivery
(Viral Trifecta); spread-worthy
content; viral marketing
Eminem, 4, 94
engaging followers, Twitter, 75
ESPN, 191, 201
"estimated reach" of ad, Facebook, 177
Ethernet, 8
Ettinger, Amber Lee ("Obama Girl"), 14,
15, 118
"evergreen" content, blogs, 84
Excel, 46
existing system pieces platform, 30–31
exporting members, email, 46

Facebook, 54–68
"about" section, 58
"admins," 57
apps (applications), 66–67
blogs and, 55, 82, 85
building your page, 56–59, 65–67
cross-leveraging marketing, 200
"de-friending," Burger King, 111–12,
203
email and, 45–46, 59, 60, 64,
186, 187
"fans" of organizations, 55, 63–65,
69, 179–80
FBML, 66–67
"feed," 55
frequency of posts, 60–61
"friends," 55
generic pages, 56–57
images and posts, 62
Insights, 59–60, 63
jump-starting marketing, 192, 194,
199, 200, 201
landing places, 58, 65–66

"like," 55, 60, 62, 67–68, 96
marketing your Facebook page,
63–65
media sources, finding, 192
mistakes in messages,
deliberate, 113
multipliers, finding, 135–36, 137–38
name for fan page, 56–57
"pages" for organizations, 55,
56–59, 65–67, 179–80, 180–83
peer pressure delivered by,
67–68, 183
picture icons, 58
"profiles" of individuals, 55, 56
sex appeal, using, 117, 120
share it, 62
soliciting comments, 61, 63
spread-worthy content, 60–63,
128
status updates, 55, 60–63, 69, 180
target audience ("who"), 65, 171–72,
173, 175, 176–77, 179, **181**,
181–83, 186
testing, 90, 128
thank-you updates, 96
tracking activity, 59–60, 63, 66
Twitter and, 69–70, 71, 72–73,
74, 80
uniform resource locators (URLs),
59, 62, 112–13
"unlike," 61
updating records, 141, 142
viral marketing and, 3, 4, 5, 6, 8, 9,
18, 19, 20
"wall," 58, 65–66
websites and, 25, 37, 41, 57, 58, 64,
171
See also Facebook advertising; mechanism for delivery
(Viral Trifecta); social media;
spread-worthy content; viral marketing
Facebook advertising, 154, 171–83,
185–87
bidding for ads, 178
budget, 64–65, 173, 177–78
click-through rates, 182, 183
complementary pages, 186
connections, 55, 176–77
cost per click (CPC), 64, 153, 173,
174, 175, 178
cost per thousand views (CPM), 64,
173, 178
echo effect, 185–87
"estimated reach" of ad, 177

"fans" of organizations, 55, 63–65, 69, 179–80
flexibility, 156
geographic location, 186, 199
Google AdWords and, 174
headlines, 57, 174
image for ads, 175–76
keywords, 172
optimizing ads, 178–79
page affinity analysis, **181**, 181–82
"pages" for organizations, 179–80, 180–83
placing your ads, 173–79
"recommended pages," 181
school, 186
target audience ("who"), 65, 171–72, 173, 175, 176–77, 179, **181**, 181–83, 186
testing, 178–79, 186–87
text for ads, 151, 174–75
time frame for ads, 177–78
workplace, 186, 201
"you," change to your page, 180–81
See also advertising; Facebook
failures as foundation for successes, 209
"fans" of organizations, Facebook, 55, 63–65, 69, 179–80
FBML, 66–67
"feed," Facebook, 55
feedback from reporters, 198
Fey, Tina, 103
"find friends," 136
finding the right multipliers, 131–39
flexibility of ads, 156
focus on results, advertising, 147–49
following, building on Twitter, 76–77
Fox, Megan, 117
frequency of
blogs posts, 82–83, 84
Facebook posts, 60–61
mail, 49–50
Twitter posts, 74
"friends," Facebook, 55
Friendster, 9
"from" line, email, 50
fun public relations tricks, 200–201

Gazoontite.com, 28
generic pages, Facebook, 56–57
geographic location, Facebook, 186, 199

Georgetown Cupcake, 79–80
Georgetowner, 188
Georgetown Patch, 188
Ghonim, Wael, 4
GIF, 150
Glee (TV show), 117
Gmail, 31, 52, 136
goals, setting your
viral marketing, 16–20, 34, 208–9
websites, 24, 31, 35, 39, 44
See also viral marketing
GoDaddy.com, 28
Godin, Seth, 90–91, 132, 204
Golden Boob Award (NBCC), 100–101
Google
jump-starting marketing, 191–92, 193
keywords, 172
media sources, finding, 191–92, 193
messages (Viral Trifecta), 117
websites and, 26
See also Google AdWords
Google AdWords, 154, 159–63
bidding for keywords, 161
click-through rates, 160, 162
cost per click (CPC), 153, 159, 162
crafting your ad, 162–63
Facebook and, 174
flexibility, 156
headlines, 160, 163
keywords, 161
links in, 160
optimizing ads, 163
partner sites, 160
target audience ("who"), 160, 162
testing, 163
text ads, 150, 159, 162–63
See also advertising; Google
Google Analytics, 42–43, 59
Google Maps, 39
Go the F*ck to Sleep (Mansbach), 104–5, 115
government health care, 103
GQ, 117
"grabber" image, 151
Green Workplace, The (Stringer), 56
grouping members, email, 46–47
Gutenberg printing press, 5

Halpern, Justin, 4
hash tags, Twitter, 71–72
headlines, 57, 151, 160, 163, 166, 167–68, 174, 195

healthcare reform, 103
Hilton, Paris, 29
Hinkler, Bert, 91
hives (subgroups of blogs), 165
Hlinko, John, 4–5, 33, 50, 91, 95, 115
HlinkoConsulting.com, 33
home page, websites, 23, 36–37,
    39, 40
hooks
    advertising, 148, 156–58
    Facebook posts, 61
    reporters and, 194–95
    Twitter posts, 74
hosting options, websites, 28, 32,
    43–44
"hot," riding existing wave, 92–95, 103
Hotmail, 31
HotOrNot.com, 118
hot people in messages, 118, 119
HTML, 29, 51, 52, 66
Huffington Post, 94
humor in messages, 98–107, 158,
    194–95
Hurson, Tim, 106
hyperlinks. *See* links
hyper-viral online campaigns, xi

Ibrahim, Ahmed, 120
icons, riding existing wave, 93–94
iFrame, 66–67
image ads, 149–50, 152
images and posts, Facebook, 62
images in ads, 166, 167, 169,
    175–76
immediate reaction to messages, 107
importing new members, email, 46
"influentials in a vacuum," 132
information architecture, 25
Insights, Facebook, 59–60, 63
InstantDomainSearch.com, 27
interesting messages. *See*
    spread-worthy content
Internet
    blogs advertising and, 164
    jump-starting marketing, 205
    memes, 94–95, 132
    messages (Viral Trifecta), 102, 105,
        113, 114
    messengers (Viral Trifecta), 129,
        131, 135
    mistakes, spreading, 113–14
    spread-worthy content and, 89–90
    viral marketing and, x, 3, 5, 7, 8, 12,
        14, 15, 16, 17
    websites and, 42

See also mechanism for delivery
    (Viral Trifecta); spread-worthy
    content; viral marketing
intuitiveness for websites, 27, 28–29
iPhones, 45
iStockphoto.com, 35, 149–50
iTunes, xii

Jackson, Bud, 157
Joomla.org, 31
joy sponges, overcoming, 101, 202–7
JPEG, 150
jump-starting marketing, 145–207
    blogs for, 185, 192, 193, 197, 199
    click-through rates, 206
    contact information, 37, 38–39, 195
    cross-leveraging marketing,
        199–200
    email for, 193, 194, 196, 200
    Facebook for, 192, 194, 199,
        200, 201
    Google for, 191–92, 193
    Internet for, 205
    joy sponges, overcoming,
        101, 202–7
    public relations (PR), 51, 157, 158,
        190–201
    spread-worthy content, 191,
        194–97
    target audience ("who"), 191–92,
        199, 201
    testing ideas, 205–6, 207
    Twitter for, 194, 200
    See also advertising; viral marketing
JustSayBlow.com, 105–6, 112–13, 158,
    196–97

keywords, 77, 161, 165, 172

Lady Gaga, 4, 65, 94
landing places, Facebook, 58, 65–66
LeftAction.com, 38, 50, 95, 180, 181,
    181, 182
Leibovitz, Annie, 35
leveraging viral technology.
    See mechanism for delivery (Viral
    Trifecta)
"lewd" humor, 104
"Life Is Short. Have an Affair"
    slogan, 114
"like," Facebook, 55, 60, 62,
    67–68, 96
Limbaugh, Rush, 95
Lindbergh, Charles, 91
LinkedIn, 9, 138

links in
  advertising, 160, 166–67
  blogs, 83, 84, 85, 166–67
  email, 43, 44, 48, 51, 133–34
  Twitter, 76, 77, 85
  websites, 36, 37, 38, 39, 44, 48
Lord of the Fries, 106, 113

MailChimp.com, 48–49
Major League Baseball, 91
Mansbach, Adam, 104–5, 115
Margulies, Josh, 157
Markman, Pacy, 17
Mashable, 62
"masked forward," 41
Maxim, 114, 191
McDonald's, 19, 110, 112
measuring advertising results, 148
mechanism for delivery
    (Viral Trifecta)
  viral marketing and, xii–xiii, 5, 7,
    8–11, *10*, 15, 21
  See also blogs; email; Facebook;
    Internet; messages (Viral
    Trifecta); messengers (Viral
    Trifecta); Twitter; viral marketing;
    websites
media sources, finding, 191–94
mega multipliers, 138–39
memes, Internet, 94–95, 132
messages (Viral Trifecta), 87–128
  blogs and, 111
  cognitive dissonance, 112
  email and, 96, 99, 100, 102, 104,
    107, 113, 115, 119, 122–28
  Google, 117
  humor in, 98–107, 158, 194–95
  Internet and, 102, 105, 113, 114
  problem, giving audience,
    108–15, 197
  sex appeal in, 15, 28, 116–21
  target audience ("who"), 104–5
  testing, 51, 52–53, 90, 122–28,
    142–43
  viral marketing and, xii, 5, 7, 13,
    15, 87
  See also mechanism for delivery
    (Viral Trifecta); messengers (Viral
    Trifecta); spread-worthy content;
    viral marketing
messengers (Viral Trifecta), 129–44
  blogs and, 134, 138
  email and, 132, 133–35, 136, 137,
    138, 140, 141, 142, 143
  Internet and, 129, 131, 135

multipliers, 131–44
  strategy, skewing to multipliers,
    140–44
  target audience ("who"), 143–44
  viral marketing and, xii, xiii, 7–8, 15
  See also mechanism for delivery
    (Viral Trifecta); messages (Viral
    Trifecta); viral marketing
Metcalfe, Robert/Metcalfe's Law, 8
Microsoft, xi, 35, 150
Middleton, Kate, 95
Miller Lite, 17
mistakes (deliberate), spreading, 113–14
MoveOn.org, xi, 181, 208
MSNBC, 120
MTV, 35–36
multipliers, 131–44
Mustafa, Isaiah, 78
MySpace, 65–66, 136
myth (biggest), viral marketing, 6

National Breast Cancer Coalition
    (NBCC), 99–101
National Lampoon, 114
naysayers, ignoring, 210
".net" domain name suffix, 27
"netroots," 12, 13
networks, power of, 8–9
news, riding existing wave, 92–93,
    94, 103
news organizations and Twitter, 85–86
news page, websites, 39, 199–200
Newsweek, 39, 92, 119
New York Times, 38, 39, 92, 168, 201
"Not Having George Bush as
    President" (Hlinko), 4–5, 91
novel messages, 90–92
NPR, 4, 117, 181

Obama, Barack (President), xi, 4,
    11–15, 103, 118
"Obama Girl" (Amber Lee Ettinger), 14,
    15, 118
offensive messages, 114–15
"Oh, oh, *oh, Canada*" campaign, 113
Old Spice Guy, 77–79, 99
Olympics wave, 93, 101
118th email test, 90, 196
ongoing narrative, building an,
    96–97
online medium focus, advertising, 148,
    156
online time of Americans, 5
open rates, email, 127
open-source systems, 30, 31, 32, 44

optimizing
  ads, 163, 168–70, 178–79
  blogs, 83–84
  jump-starting marketing, 191
O'Reilly, Bill, 102
".org" domain name suffix, 27–28
overcoming inertia, messages, 109–10

page affinity analysis, Facebook, **181**, 181–82
"pages" for organizations, Facebook, 55, 56–59, 65–67, 179–80, 180–83
Palin, Bristol, 102
Palin, Sarah, 4, 103, 115, 172, 175
Panetta, Mike, 92–93
partner sites, Google AdWords, 160
"past performance," advertising, 152
Paterson, David, 103
patterns and routines, messages, 109, 110
paying for advertising, 152–54
peer pressure power, 9–11, 10, 37, 67–68, 183, 206–7
People for the Ethical Treatment of Animals (PETA), 120
"perceived experts," 132
PerezHilton.com, 29, 151
personalization, 43–44, 47–48, 51
Photoshop, 35, 149
piggybacking on existing URL, 26
pitching the reporters, 197–98, 200
pixels, 150
placement of ads, 152–53
places to advertise, choosing, 154–56
placing your ads, Facebook, 173–79
Planet of the Grapes, 106, 113
Planned Parenthood, 181, **181**
planning, viral marketing, 6, 20, 188–89
platforms, websites, 25, 26, 28, 29–33, 42
Playboy, 191
"plug and play," 30, 34, 35
power users, social media, 4
Presley, Elvis, 4
press coverage, websites, 39
Primetime Emmy Award for Outstanding Commercial, 78
prioritizing
  advertising, 148
  media sources, 192–93
  websites content, 39, 40
problem, giving your audience, 108–15, 197

"profiles" of individuals, Facebook, 55, 56
progress reports, 96
public relations (PR), 51, 157, 158, 190–201
publishers, advertising, 150, 155–56
puns in messages, 105–6, 112–13
Purple Cow (Godin), 90–91, 132, 204
putting it all together, 208–10

quotes for public relations, 195–96

radio advertising, 148, 158
Rapleaf.com, 135–36
read and spread. *See* viral marketing
"recommended pages," Facebook, 181
recycling mode, blogs, 84, 86
Red Sox, 110
registering domain names, 28, 41
reporters, following, Twitter, 77
Republican convention of 2008, 102
results, focus on, 147–49
"retweets," Twitter, 70, 75, 128, 136–37
"revelatory" humor, 102
"Rickroll," 94–95, 108, 195, 196
riding existing wave, 92–95, 103, 158
Rihanna, 4
Robinson, Jackie, 91

Said, Khaled, 4
Salsa (platform), 31, 44, 48
Sanders, Bernie, 181, **181**, 182
Saturday Night Live (TV show), 101, 103, 132
schadenfreude, 113
school, Facebook, 186
"scraped" emails, 39
Seoul Food, 106, 113
setting your goals. *See* goals, setting your
sex appeal, messages, 15, 28, 116–21
"Shag the Vote" campaign, 113
Shakira, 117
"share-friendly," websites, 24, 40–42, 44
share it, Facebook, 62
Shatner, William, 205
"ShitMyDadSays" (Halpern), 4
shout-outs, 96–97
Simon, Scott, 4
Snagit, 35, 149
"sneezers," messengers, 132
SnorgTees.com, 38

social media
  blogs and, 84–86
  viral marketing and, xii–xiii, 3–5, 6,
    7, 9–11, *10*, 13, 15
  See also Facebook; Twitter; viral
    marketing
soliciting comments, Facebook, 61, 63
Southeast Asia, 9
spam, 39, 48, 52–53
Spam Arrest, 52
SpamCheck, 52–53
Spears, Jamie Lynn, 102
Sports Illustrated, 114, 191
spread-worthy content, 89–97
  blogs, 82–84
  email, 49–53, 124–28
  Facebook, 60–63, 128
  Internet, 89–90
  jump-starting marketing, 191,
    194–97
  novel messages, 90–92
  ongoing narrative, building an,
    96–97
  progress reports, 96
  public relations (PR), 191, 194–97
  riding existing wave, 92–95,
    103, 158
  shout-outs, 96–97
  target audience ("who"), 90, 95
  Twitter, 74–76, 128
  villains, using, 95, 100–101,
    103, 158
  websites, 23, 24, 25, 36–40
  See also messages (Viral Trifecta);
    viral marketing
"squeaky wheel gets the grease,"
  108–15
"standard forward," 41
Starbucks, 67
Star Wars (film), 6
status updates, Facebook, 55, 60–63,
  69, 180
Stefani, Gwen, 94
strategy, skewing to multipliers,
  140–44
Stringer, Leigh, 56
subgroups (email), sending to, 46–47
subject line, email, 50–51, 123,
  126, 127
subscribing, email, 48
success of viral marketing, xi–xii, xiii
synching up timing and location of
  public relations, 199
synergistic effect, jump-starting
  marketing, 199–200

target audience ("who")
  action desired ("what") of, 17,
    19–20, 34
  advertising, 155, 189
  blogs advertising, 170
  demographics of, 18–19
  email, 104
  Facebook, 65, 171–72, 173, 175,
    176–77, 179, **181**, 181–83, 186
  Google AdWords, 160, 162
  jump-starting marketing, 191–92,
    199, 201
  messages (Viral Trifecta), 104–5
  messengers (Viral Trifecta), 143–44
  problem, giving audience,
    108–15, 197
  spread-worthy content, 90, 95
  Twitter, 104
  viral marketing and, 17, 18–20, 34
  websites, 27, 34, 36, 37
  See also viral marketing
TechCrunch, 111
technology. *See* mechanism for
  delivery (Viral Trifecta)
TechSmith.com, 35, 149
teenage pregnancy, 102
telephone, contacting using, 194
"Telling Dick Cheney to Shut the Hell
  Up" (Hlinko), 95
"Telling Rush Limbaugh He's Full of
  Crap" (Hlinko), 95
"Telling Sarah Palin She's Full of Crap"
  (Hlinko), 115
template-based systems,
  websites, 33
testing
  advertising, 154–55, 163, 168–70,
    178–79, 186–87
  blogs advertising, 168–70
  email, 51, 52–53, 90, 122–28,
    142–43, 155
  Facebook, 90, 128, 178–79, 186–87
  Google AdWords, 163
  jump-starting marketing,
    205–6, 207
  messages (Viral Trifecta), 51, 52–53,
    90, 122–28, 142–43
  Twitter, 90, 128
text ads, 150–51, 152, 159, 162–63,
  174–75
text vs. HTML, email, 51, 52
thanking messengers, 134–35,
  137, 138
thank-you updates, Facebook, 96
"theater of culture," 109–10

themes for, websites, 30–31, 32, 34
Think Better (Hurson), 106
Time, 114
time duration, paying, 152–53, 154,
   165–66
time for blogs, 83, 86
time frame for ads, Facebook,
   177–78
timeliness (riding existing wave),
   92–95, 103, 158
TinyUrl.com, 76
titles (optimizing for searching),
   blogs, 84
TLC, 80
T-Mobile, 95
tools. *See* mechanism for delivery
   (Viral Trifecta)
tracking activity
   blogs, 84
   email, 48–49, 133–35, 136
   Facebook, 59–60, 63, 66
   multipliers across platforms, 141–42
   websites, 42–43
"trending" topics, Twitter, 76, 92
trends and adjusting marketing,
   143–44
TV advertising, 148, 156–57, 158
".tv" domain name suffix, 28
"Twistory," 78
Twitter, 69–80
   advertising on, 73, 76
   blogs and, 71, 82, 85–86
   community building on, 71–73
   cross-leveraging marketing, 200
   email and, 45–46, 77
   engaging followers, 75
   Facebook and, 69–70, 71, 72–73,
      74, 80
   following, building, 76–77
   frequency of posts, 74
   hash tags, 71–72
   "hook" of posts, 74
   jump-starting marketing,
      194, 200
   keywords, searching for, 77
   links in, 76, 77, 85
   multipliers, finding, 135–36, 136–37
   news organizations and, 85–86
   reporters, following, 77
   "retweets," 70, 75, 128, 136–37
   spread-worthy content, 74–76, 128
   target audience ("who"), 104
   testing, 90, 128
   "trending" topics, 76, 92
   "tweets," 69

uniform resource locators
   (URLs), 76
updating records, 141, 142
viral marketing and, 3, 4, 5, 9
websites and, 25, 41, 75–76, 77
See also mechanism for delivery
   (Viral Trifecta); social media;
   spread-worthy content; viral marketing
TypePad.com, 33, 34, 35, 82

uniform resource locators (URLs)
   blogs, 84
   Facebook, 59, 62, 112–13
   Twitter, 76
   websites, 23, 26–29, 41, 58, 59
"unlike," Facebook, 61
unsubscribing, email, 48
updating content, blogs, 82–83, 84
updating records and multipliers,
   140–42
Uptown Valet, 119–20
urgency of going viral, 3–15

Vagina Monologues, The (play), 115
Vertical Response, 48–49
videos, messages, 106
views, cost per thousand (CPM), 64,
   153, 154, 156, 165–66, 169, 173,
   178
villains, using, 95, 100–101, 103, 158
Vince the ShamWow! Guy
   (infomercial), 94
viral marketing, xi–20, 208–10
   data driven, 209–10
   failures as foundation for
      successes, 209
   myth (biggest) about, 6
   naysayers, ignoring, 210
   networks, power of, 8–9
   online time of Americans, 5
   peer pressure power, 9–11, *10*, 37,
      67–68, 183, 206–7
   planning, 6, 20, 188–89
   putting it all together, 208–10
   success of, xi–xii, xiii
   urgency of going viral, 3–15
   Viral Trifecta, xii, 1, 6–15, 209
   See also advertising; goals, setting
      your; jump-starting marketing;
      mechanism for delivery
      (Viral Trifecta); messages (Viral
      Trifecta); messengers (Viral Trifec-
      ta); social media; spread-worthy
      content; target audience ("who")

Wait Wait . . . Don't Tell Me! (NPR show), 181, **181**
"wall," Facebook, 58, 65–66
Wall Street Journal, 117, 120
Walmart, xi
Washington, DC voting rights, 93, 101
Washington Post, 38, 92, 188
"We Are All Khaled Said" (Ghonim), 4
websites, 23–44
   "about" page, 37–38
   advertising and, 148
   all-in-one back-end platforms,
      31–32, 43–44, 48, 49
   blog-based platforms, 32–33
   blogs and, 26, 29, 32, 33, 34, 35,
      81, 82, 84
   collecting data, 42–43
   ".com" domain name suffix, 26, 27
   consultants for, 24–26, 30,
      33–34, 41
   contact information, 37, 38–39
   cross-leveraging marketing,
      199–200
   custom-built platforms, 30
   databases, 31, 32, 43–44
   designing, 24, 25, 26, 31, 33–36
   domain names, 26–28, 41, 57
   download caution, 35
   email and, 23, 31, 32, 33, 39, 41,
      43, 44
   existing system pieces platform,
      30–31
   Facebook and, 25, 37, 41, 57, 58,
      64, 171
   goals for, 24, 31, 35, 39, 44
   Google Analytics, 42–43, 59
   Google and, 26
   home page, 23, 36–37, 39, 40
   hosting options, 28, 32, 43–44
   information architecture, 25
   Internet and, 42
   intuitiveness for, 27, 28–29
   links in, 36, 37, 38, 39, 44, 48
   news page, 39, 199–200
   open-source systems, 30, 31, 32, 44

   personalization, 43–44
   platforms, 25, 26, 28, 29–33, 42
   prioritizing content, 39, 40
   registering domain names,
      28, 41
   "share-friendly," 24, 40–42, 44
   spread-worthy content, 23, 24, 25,
      36–40
   target audience ("who"), 27, 34, 36,
      37
   template-based systems, 33
   themes for, 30–31, 32, 34
   tracking activity, 42–43
   Twitter and, 25, 41, 75–76, 77
   uniform resource locators (URLs),
      23, 26–29, 41, 58, 59
   widgets, 41–42
   See also mechanism for delivery
      (Viral Trifecta); spread-worthy
      content; viral marketing
Weeds (TV show), 181, **181**, 182
"what" (action desired of target
   audience), 17, 19–20, 34
WhiteHouse.gov/.com, 27
"who." *See* target audience ("who")
Whopper Sacrifice, 111–12, 203
widgets, 41–42
will.i.am, 11–12, 14, 15
William, Prince, 95
"Wind Tunnel" brainstorm, 106–7
WordPress.com/.org, 32, 33, 34,
   44, 82
workplace, Facebook, 186, 201

Yahoo!, 28, 41, 52, 136
Yankees, 110
Yankelovich, xiii
"Yes We Can" (video), 12
"you" change, Facebook, 180–81
YouTube, xii, 12, 13, 23, 78, 94, 95,
   99, 102

Zuckerberg, Mark, 13, 46, 54
Zuckerberg, Randi, 62
Zuniga, Markos Moulitsas, 12

ABOUT THE AUTHOR

Mary Helen Stringer

John Hlinko has been long recognized as an innovator and "Buzz Czar" on the grassroots marketing front, using emerging technology and creative communications to achieve maximum results within constrained budgets. He has been covered by nearly all the major U.S. broadcast and print news outlets, and has been quoted as a grassroots expert in more than a dozen books ranging from *Power Public Relations* to *Burning at the Grassroots*.

Hlinko has earned a number of awards and accolades, including being named one of the top five "PR Professionals of the Year" by *PRWeek* and one of world's top 25 "individuals, organizations, and companies that are having the greatest impact on the way the Internet is changing politics" by the World Forum on e-Democracy.

He has worked with some of the biggest breakout viral success stories, starting with MoveOn.org in its earliest days and a "draft Obama" effort to build support for Barack Obama in advance of his presidential run. He has also worked extensively on the corporate side, with a range of Fortune 500 clients such as Walmart, Disney, and Microsoft.

Hlinko is a highly sought after speaker who has addressed hundreds of groups, in settings ranging from small classrooms to audiences of thousands, and in locales ranging from San Francisco to Warsaw to Istanbul. He is the founder of Left Action, a network of more than a million progressive activists, and ActForLove.org, an activist-focused dating site with the slogan "Take Action, Get Action." He holds a BA from Wesleyan University and a master's degree from Harvard.

He lives in New York with his wife, Leigh, and his daughters, Kate and Ali.